Handbook of Incentive Measures for Biodiversity

Design and Implementation

ORGANISATION FOR ECONOMIC CO-OPERATION AND DEVELOPMENT

ORGANISATION FOR ECONOMIC CO-OPERATION AND DEVELOPMENT

Pursuant to Article 1 of the Convention signed in Paris on 14th December 1960, and which came into force on 30th September 1961, the Organisation for Economic Co-operation and Development (OECD) shall promote policies designed:

- to achieve the highest sustainable economic growth and employment and a rising standard of living in Member countries, while maintaining financial stability, and thus to contribute to the development of the world economy;
- to contribute to sound economic expansion in Member as well as non-member countries in the process of economic development; and
- to contribute to the expansion of world trade on a multilateral, non-discriminatory basis in accordance with international obligations.

The original Member countries of the OECD are Austria, Belgium, Canada, Denmark, France, Germany, Greece, Iceland, Ireland, Italy, Luxembourg, the Netherlands, Norway, Portugal, Spain, Sweden, Switzerland, Turkey, the United Kingdom and the United States. The following countries became Members subsequently through accession at the dates indicated hereafter: Japan (28th April 1964), Finland (28th January 1969), Australia (7th June 1971), New Zealand (29th May 1973), Mexico (18th May 1994), the Czech Republic (21st December 1995), Hungary (7th May 1996), Poland (22nd November 1996) and Korea (12th December 1996). The Commission of the European Communities takes part in the work of the OECD (Article 13 of the OECD Convention).

Publié en français sous le titre :

MANUEL DE PROTECTION DE LA BIODIVERSITÉ
Conception et mise en œuvre des mesures incitatives

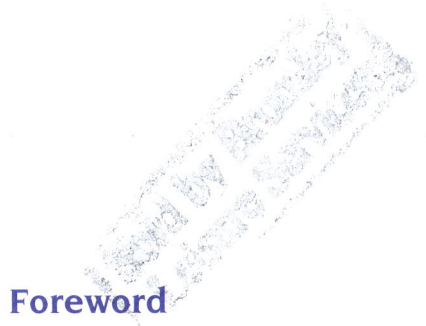

Foreword

The OECD Working Group on Economic Aspects of Biodiversity undertook in 1996 to "fulfil the need of OECD Member countries for pragmatic policy guidance regarding the implementation of incentive measures for the conservation and the sustainable use of biological diversity". This publication is the main result of those efforts. It is a practical handbook to assist policy makers in the design and implementation of appropriate incentive measures for the effective management of biodiversity. It synthesises the lessons learned from the experiences of OECD Member countries in the use of a variety of incentive measures (as described in 22 case studies), and combines this with a coherent conceptual framework to develop comprehensive guidance on the policies available for preventing biodiversity loss.

The handbook is also part of the development of an OECD-wide horizontal programme on sustainable development, one of five priority areas identified by the Secretary-General in 1998. In addition, it corresponds with the main recommendations of the report of the Secretary-General's High Level Advisory Group on the Environment, which emphasised the need for greater policy integration and increased resource efficiency.

In a wider sense, the handbook also provides an important contribution to international efforts to implement the Convention on Biological Diversity. It forms the basis of OECD efforts to comply with Article IV/10A of the Decisions adopted by the Fourth Conference of Parties to the Convention on Biological Diversity (Bratislava, 4-15 May 1998). This decision requests the Executive Secretary of the Convention on Biological Diversity:

> *To prepare in collaboration with the Organisation for Economic Development and Co-operation (OECD), the World Conservation Union (IUCN) and other relevant organizations, a background paper containing further analysis of the design and implementation of incentive measures for the conservation and sustainable use of biodiversity… with the aim of developing guidance to parties.*

The handbook was prepared by Jan Horst Keppler and Helen Mountford of the OECD Secretariat under the guidance of the Working Group on Economic Aspects of Biodiversity. It is published under the responsibility of the Secretary-General of the OECD.

OECD 1999

Table of Contents

OECD 1999

List of boxes

I.   About this *Handbook* and How to Use it

Why a *handbook* on incentive measures for biodiversity?

Biological diversity is a valuable asset for both present and future generations, as well as an important basis for sustainable development. It encompasses the conservation of a variety of different species, genetic variability among individuals within each species, and the existence of a variety of ecosystems. Conserving this diversity is essential for human economic development – it provides food, energy, raw materials, industrial chemicals, and medicines, as well as important social and cultural benefits.

However, because many of the benefits of biodiversity conservation accrue to the public as a whole, and because of information, market and government failures, biodiversity resources are often utilised at levels that are not sustainable. As a result, species extinction caused by human activities continue at an alarming rate, particularly for mammals and amphibians. Incentive measures are required to internalise the full costs of biodiversity loss in the activities that lead to this loss, and to provide the necessary information, support and incentives to sustainably use or conserve biological diversity. The Convention on Biological Diversity therefore recognises the importance of incentive measures and encourages all Contracting Parties to "... adopt economically and socially sound measures that act as incentives for the conservation and sustainable use of components of biological diversity" (Article 11).

How to use this *Handbook*?

This *Handbook* is designed to assist policy makers and their advisors in the design and the implementation of incentive measures for encouraging the conservation and sustainable use of biological resources. Different policies are applicable depending on the ecosystems in need of protection and the sectors that are exerting pressure on the biological resources. In addition to providing guidance on how to implement incentive measures, the *Handbook* also describes which measures are most suitable for which ecosystems and sectors, and what the drawbacks of each incentive measure are and how these can be overcome through utilising a combination of instruments. The recommendations are drawn from the practical experiences of OECD Member countries in implementing such incentive measures, presented in twenty-two case studies (see Annex II for a summary of the case studies).

The *Handbook* can be used to browse and to search for topics of interest, such as a specific ecosystem or a specific incentive measure. It can also be used as a gradually expanding compendium in which the discussion of issues relating to the development of policies to tackle biodiversity depletion becomes increasingly deeper and more detailed. The annexes provide further information and orientation. Perhaps the quickest and easiest way for a policy maker to use the *Handbook* would be to go directly to Chapter II and simply follow the checklist provided there of the most important issues that need to be addressed in the design and implementation of any incentive measure to encourage the sustainable use or conservation of biodiversity.

However, while the checklist represents a condensed version of the policy advice contained in the *Handbook*, this procedure is not recommended. The rest of the *Handbook* provides important information on the context and environment (both political and physical) in which incentive measures are applied. Thus, Chapter III gives an overview of the context in which this work has been undertaken, and Chapter IV a general perspective on biodiversity values and incentive measures for its protection. Chapter V describes the characteristics of the main ecosystems in OECD countries. Chapters VI and VII form the main part of the *Handbook*, outlining respectively the processes required for successful implementation of incentive measures and the lessons drawn from the case studies about the different incentive measures that can be used.

The first Annex describes the structure of the "Framework for Case Studies", under which each of the case studies provided by Member countries was prepared. This is followed by Annex II, which provides an overview of the common Framework used to develop the twenty-two case studies undertaken by Member countries and short summaries of each of the studies with contact details for further information. Annex III is a glossary of important terms, with references to the sections of the *Handbook* where they can be found.

What this *Handbook* is likely to tell you?

Biodiversity provides a range of goods and services to human society, including those with privately-appropriable values and those with public ones. Because of the intrinsic complexity of biological diversity and the pressures that act upon it, designing incentive measures to realise both the public and private values associated with it presents policy makers with unique challenges. This *Handbook* identifies some of the incentive measures that can be used, the experiences OECD Member countries have had with their application, and the best strategies for designing and implementing the most appropriate measures for the pressures faced by different ecosystems, and arising from different sectors.

Many biological resources can be used for economically productive purposes in a sustainable manner. Where this is possible, both the privately-appropriable values of the resources and the public benefits of their continued existence can be realised. In such cases, the most appropriate incentive measures to ensure that their use does not lead to biodiversity depletion are the creation of markets and the assignment of well-defined property rights to realise the full private benefits of the resources, in combination with regulations and standards to proscribe the allowable levels and types of use. In addition, this requires the removal or reform of adverse incentives which induce actors to use the resources at unsustainable levels.

Such measures can include policies as diverse as the implementation of a certification or eco-labelling scheme to create a market for biodiversity-friendly products and services, the attachment of a legal covenant to a piece of land specifying what activities can or cannot be undertaken there, or the removal of subsidies for agriculture or development which encourage the clearance of biologically-rich areas. Where these measures are insufficient on their own to induce the desired behaviour, positive incentives are needed in the form of support for biodiversity-conserving activities or the creation of environmental funds for the express purpose of supporting such activities. These can help to bridge the profitability gap between sustainable activities and unsustainable alternatives, and are also the most likely to gain support from local communities and the private sector.

In some cases, sustainable use of the resources will not be possible. This will be the case, for example, where a species is depleted to such an extent that any consumptive use may contribute to its potential extinction or where ensuring compliance with restrictions for sustainable use is either not possible or would be excessively expensive. In such cases, pure preservation measures will be required instead. These generally require restrictions on access to the biological resources or ecosystems, such as through the development of natural parks to protect ecosystems or habitats, or implementing regulations which prohibit the harvesting or other use of a particularly threatened or endangered species. A general message that arises from the *Handbook* is that well-defined property rights and economic incentives should be utilised wherever possible to realise sustainable use, and regulations, access restrictions and subsidisation of sustainable use wherever necessary.

Some considerations apply to *all* incentive measures. Because of the range of stakeholders concerned with the conservation or use of biological resources, and the complexity of the systems involved, it is important to strengthen scientific and technical capacity, to involve all the relevant stakeholders in the decision-making processes, to ensure that the available information about the resources and the pressures on them is transmitted to the appropriate parties, and to strengthen or construct appropriate institutions for handling the policy decisions, the implementation and enforcement of the incentive measures and the monitoring of the biological resources. While all of these activities can be seen as incentive measures in their own right to enable or encourage the sustainable use or conservation of biological diversity, they are also essential framework conditions for the successful implementation of any of the other incentive measures listed above. As such, they provide an important foundation to build a coherent and successful policy mix upon.

Even where these essential contextual framework conditions are in place, often a mix of incentive measures will be required to realise the full value of biodiversity. This is particularly important for biodiversity policies because of the uncertainties surrounding the pressures on the resources and the effects on the resources of these pressures, as well as the number of actors involved. Because of this complexity, it is often difficult to design a single policy instrument that will successfully provide the right incentives for the sustainable use or conservation of the resources by all the relevant actors. Instead, it is often preferable to employ a range of incentive measures in order to address all the pressures and actors and which, through some overlap in the measures, can provide essential backup in case any one measure fails to provide sufficient incentives.

The Expert Group on Economic Aspects of Biodiversity and the OECD Secretariat, which together prepared this *Handbook*, hope that it will contribute to facilitating the understanding of the issues surrounding biodiversity depletion and the implementation of appropriate incentive measures. In the final instance, no conceptual guidance can substitute for the political will to conserve and sustainably use biodiversity. The impressive engagement of OECD Member countries demonstrated by the provision of twenty-two case studies, in combination with the conceptual work of the Secretariat, however, constitutes a substantial step forward towards the protection of biodiversity and the implementation of the Convention on Biological Diversity.

II. Checklist for the Implementation of Incentive Measures

A short overview of the issues and questions which have to be considered by any decision-maker when designing incentive measures for the sustainable use or conservation of biodiversity is presented below. The checklist is designed to help policy makers to plan a comprehensive programme for designing an appropriate mix of incentive measures to address pressures on biodiversity. In particular, it is intended to assist in the formation of incentives to reduce unregulated open access to biological resources and to close the profitability gap between the unsustainable and sustainable use of these resources. It stands at the beginning of an extensive discussion of the design and implementation of appropriate incentive measures presented in the following chapters.

1. What is the problem? What are the manifest symptoms?

2. What are the proximate causes of the problem? What are the underlying economic and political factors that result in these causes?

3. Has awareness of the issues been sufficiently developed?

4. Which information gaps exist? How can they be addressed?

5. Have the biodiversity components been valued? How can biodiversity valuation be efficiently used to further policy objectives?

6. Who are the relevant actors and stakeholders that are likely to loose or gain from the implementation of an incentive measure? How can they be included in the process most usefully?

7. Which institutions or individuals have the relevant competencies for designing the appropriate incentive measures, as well as for follow-up monitoring and assessment, and should be consulted?

8. Can the problem be fully addressed by ensuring sustainable use of the resources? To what extent is outright protection necessary instead?

9. Which mix of incentive measures will be most effective in addressing the main aspects of the problem. What are the costs and distributional impacts?

10. Is appropriate technical and scientific capacity available? How can it be generated?

11. Do existing institutions correspond to the geographical extent as well as the scope of the biodiversity policy problem?

12. What problems of monitoring and enforcement will arise?

13. Are distributional arrangements (such as compensation measures) necessary? Can they be designed to help reduce enforcement costs?

14. What review and monitoring mechanisms are in place? Does the implementation process follow an appropriately self-reflexive and circular framework of review rather than a linear one (see Box VI.1)?

III. A *Handbook* for Practical Policy Advice

This *Handbook* aims to provide practical policy advice for decision-makers concerned with the conservation and the sustainable use of biodiversity. It continues the work of the OECD Expert Group on Economic Aspects of Biodiversity "on the identification of economically and socially sound incentives for the conservation and sustainable use of biological diversity with a focus on market-based economic instruments and with attention to social concerns and needs, cost-effectiveness, valuation, and institutional arrangements", as expressed in the Group's mandate. It emphasises the role of barriers to the adoption of incentive measures and the elimination of incentives which promote activities exerting pressure on biological diversity (adverse incentives).

The development of the *Handbook* is also part of the OECD horizontal work programme on sustainable development (OECD, 1998*a*), which is one of five priority areas for the Organisation. The conservation and the sustainable use of biodiversity is, of course, in itself an intrinsic part of sustainable development. In a more specific sense, much of the work of the OECD Expert Group on Economic Aspects of Biodiversity is directly related to one of the focus areas within the OECD's sustainable development programme – the removal of environmentally adverse incentives and the appropriate pricing of natural resources. The focus of the *Handbook* also corresponds with the main recommendations of the report of the Secretary-General's High-Level Advisory Group on the Environment which emphasise the need for increasing resource efficiency and policy integration.

The *Handbook* presents a synthesis of the insights and experiences of implementing incentive measures that stem from three distinct sources: first and foremost, the experiences presented in the twenty-two case studies provided by OECD Member countries; second, the insights formulated in *Saving Biological Diversity: Economic Incentives* (OECD, 1996); and third, the work of the Expert Group during its mandate in the period 1997-1998. The case studies have been prepared according to the guidance presented in the document "Incentive Measures to Promote the Conservation and the Sustainable Use of Biodiversity: Framework for Case Studies" (OECD, 1997*a*) which was prepared by the Expert Group for this purpose (see Annex I for an overview

OECD 1999

of the Framework). Ultimately, it has been possible to draw policy conclusions from these case studies because they are comparable under this common framework, when otherwise they would have remained isolated, single incidences without any generalisable meaning. Close co-operation has at all stages been maintained with the Secretariat of the Convention on Biological Diversity, which has chosen to base its own case study work on the "Framework for Case Studies".

The twenty-two case studies (see Box III.1) which form the basis of the policy advice presented here cover the following ecosystems: coastal zones, marine ecosystems, terrestrial ecosystems, forests, inland fresh-water ecosystems, mountainous and submountainous regions, grass- and rangelands, and arid and semiarid areas. Each case study analyses the interaction of at least one of these ecosystems with one or more of the following economic sectors: tourism, fisheries, road transport, agriculture, forestry, land-use, shipping and industry. The intent of the *Handbook* is to combine the richness of the case study experiences with the rigour of analysis developed in *Saving Biological Diversity* in order to arrive at policy advice on the implementation of incentive measures which is based on a coherent intellectual framework, while at the same time providing practical and flexible guidance for overcoming the real-world obstacles that obstruct either the introduction or the effective working of incentive measures for the conservation and the sustainable use of biodiversity.

1. A wide and diverse audience

As the *Handbook* has been prepared on the basis of case studies from OECD Member countries, and under the responsibility of the OECD Expert Group for Economic Aspects of Biodiversity, its primary focus is to facilitate the task of policy-makers in Member countries in organising the implementation of incentive measures for the conservation and the sustainable use of biodiversity.

At the same time, the *Handbook* is also aimed at a larger audience, both inside and outside of OECD Member countries. This audience comprises all the stakeholders involved in the processes leading up to the implementation of incentive measures: the media, non-governmental organisations, consultants, advisors, economists, biologists, ecologists, users and managers of biodiversity, including the relevant industries and commercial companies. The implementation of incentive measures for the conservation and the sustainable use of biodiversity requires the involvement of policy-makers on the one hand and wider sections of civil society on the other. Its success will depend on processes set in motion and supervised by policy makers, but involving a wide range of stakeholders. The greater the extent to which all participants rely on a common conceptual framework, the easier it will be to set such processes in motion.

Box III.1. Case studies undertaken for this *Handbook*

(See Annex II for a summary of each case study)

Country	Case study title
Australia	A Revolving Fund for Biodiversity Conservation in Australia
Austria I	Economic Incentive Measures in the Creation of the National Park Neusiedler See – Seewinkel
Austria II	The Austrian Programme on Environmentally Sound and Sustainable Agriculture: Experiences and Consequences of Sustainable Use of Biodiversity in Austrian Agriculture
Canada I	Revealing the Economic Value of Biodiversity: A New Incentive Measure to Conserve and Protect It
Canada II	Using the Income Tax Act of Canada to Promote Biodiversity and Sensitive Lands Conservation
Denmark	Economic Incentives for the Transformation of Privately Cultivated Forest Areas into Strict (Untouched) Forest Reserves
Finland	The Act of the Financing of Sustainable Forestry and the Development of Forest Certification
France	A Cost-Benefit Analysis of Biodiversity Conservation Programmes in the Garonne Valley
Germany	UNESCO Biosphere Reserves Schorfheide-Chorin and Rhön
Greece	Incentives for the Conservation of the Nesting Grounds of the Sea Turtle *Caretta caretta* in Laganas Bay, Zakynthos, Greece
Japan	The Case of Oze Area: Case Study on the Japanese Experience Concerning Economic Aspects of Conserving Biodiversity
Korea	Korean Experiences Relating to the Conservation of Biodiversity in Mount Chiri, with Special Attention to the Poaching of Bears
Mexico	Incitations Economiques pour la Protection des Especes de la Vie Sauvage au Mexique: Le cas de l'Espece O*vis canadensis*
Netherlands I	Green Investment Funds: Organic Farming
Netherlands II	Green Investment Funds: PIM Project
New Zealand	Conservation of the Pae O Te Rangi Area
Norway	Valuation of Benefits Connected to Conservation or Improvement of Environmental Quality in Local Watercourses in Norway
Poland	The Implementation of Economic Incentive Measures to Promote the Conservation and Sustainable Use of Biodiversity in the Biebrza Valley, with Special Attention to the Biebrza National Park
Turkey	The Development of Appropriate Methods for Community Forestry in Turkey
UK	Heathland Management in the UK
US	US Experiences with Incentive Measures to Promote the Conservation of Wetlands
OECD	Individual Transferable Quotas as an Incentive Measure for the Conservation and the Sustainable Use of Marine Biodiversity

Two additional aspects have to be particularly highlighted in this context. First, the conservation and the sustainable use of biodiversity is a global task. Links through trade and investment and the structural changes they cause, the mutual reliance on preserving a pool of constantly renewed genetic resources, the common commitment to conserving species and ecosystems which are considered part of the world's natural heritage even if they are managed under the sovereign rights of a nation state all ensure that biodiversity is a global issue. In addition, many of the world's most biologically diverse areas are outside of the boundaries of OECD Member countries. In accordance with the importance given to the outreach to non-Member countries,[1] the Handbook is thus designed to be useful also to key actors in non-Member countries. The special focus on the building of capacity and the heightened attention to the performance of existing institutions are a direct result of this effort to have the final product appeal to a wide and diverse audience in and beyond OECD Member countries.

Last and certainly not least, this Handbook is designed to be a useful input to the work of the Conference of the Parties of the Convention on Biological Diversity and the Secretariat of the Convention. Co-operation has been highly successful in the past to the extent that work by the Expert Group such as the "Framework for Case Studies" could be directly adopted by the Secretariat for its work on case studies from non-OECD Member countries. Despite any differences in practice, the experiences of OECD and non-OECD countries are thus comparable for purposes of analytical work. This will enhance the usefulness of the Handbook for non-Member countries, even though it is based solely on case studies from OECD Member countries.

Decision III/18 of the Conference of the Parties, which recognises the OECD as an Expert Organisation in the area of incentive measures, has helped this mutually beneficial relationship. The ecosystem approach, the large number of possible instruments and incentive measures examined, and the use of a flexible approach adapted to a wide range of institutional realities are all designed to contribute to making the Handbook part of a successful joint effort in the future. Decision IV/10 requested the OECD co-operate with the CBD Secretariat and the IUCN to prepare a background report on incentive measures, in whose fulfilment this Handbook will play an important part.

2. Building on prior work and learning from experience

The twenty-two case studies provided by OECD Member countries are mainly based on their different experiences with the implementation of incentive measures for the conservation or sustainable use of biodiversity. They describe incentive measures as diverse as environmental charges, the removal of adverse subsidies, the assignment of property rights, the valuation of environmental goods and services, and the creation of environmental funds. They cover all major ecosystems and apply to economic activities reaching from tourism to agriculture, and from fisheries to industry.

The structure of the "Framework for Case Studies" with individual modules on underlying causes, adverse incentives and economic valuation and with a focus on ecosystems, information and the context of implementation reflects the conceptual work of the Expert Group. The dynamic structure of the framework provides the ability to integrate subsequent cycles of monitoring, assessment and the adaptation of incentive measures.

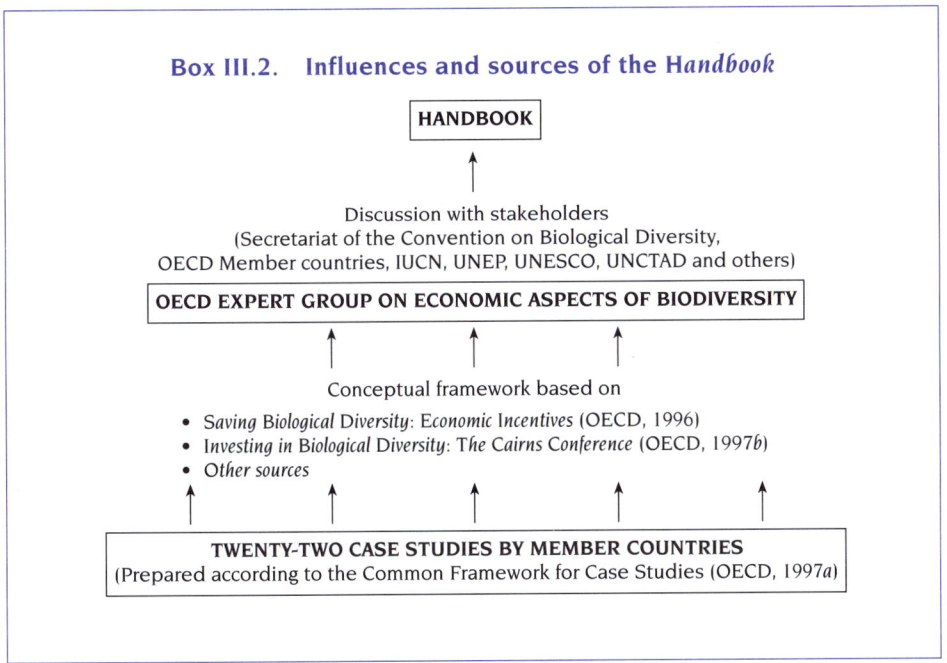

Box III.2. Influences and sources of the *Handbook*

HANDBOOK

Discussion with stakeholders
(Secretariat of the Convention on Biological Diversity,
OECD Member countries, IUCN, UNEP, UNESCO, UNCTAD and others)

OECD EXPERT GROUP ON ECONOMIC ASPECTS OF BIODIVERSITY

Conceptual framework based on
- *Saving Biological Diversity: Economic Incentives* (OECD, 1996)
- *Investing in Biological Diversity: The Cairns Conference* (OECD, 1997b)
- *Other sources*

TWENTY-TWO CASE STUDIES BY MEMBER COUNTRIES
(Prepared according to the Common Framework for Case Studies (OECD, 1997a)

The conceptual structure of the *Handbook*, as well as of the framework for the case studies, relies on the prior conclusions of the Expert Group as formulated in *Saving Biological Diversity: Economic Incentives* (OECD, 1996) and *Investing in Biological Diversity: The Cairns Conference* (OECD, 1997b). Both brought together the insights of some of the leading researchers in the field of biological diversity – economists as well as ecologists, conceptualists as well as practitioners – and developed a coherent framework which forms the intellectual basis of this effort. The conference in Cairns also extended beyond OECD countries by including participants from non-

Member countries, thus setting an important precedent for future work of the OECD Expert Group to be positioned in a perspective of outreach to and involvement of non-Member countries.

Saving Biological Diversity: Economic Incentives established an overview of the economic aspects of the problem of biodiversity loss. It provides important definitions and data on the status and the trends of biological diversity, describes the causes of biodiversity loss, and discusses the economic instruments that could be utilised to counter these losses.

It also introduced the fundamental distinction between proximate causes of biodiversity loss and the underlying economic forces that result in these causes. Proximate causes of biodiversity loss include habitat destruction, the unsustainable exploitation of wild species, the introduction of alien species, homogenisation, pollution and global environmental change, while the underlying causes behind these are market or government failures, insufficient information and the lack of clearly-defined property rights. It is these underlying causes which need to be addressed by appropriate incentive measures in order to achieve the most effective results in terms of biodiversity conservation or sustainable use (OECD, 1996; 43-65). Box III.3 below provides an overview of some of the different types of underlying causes and the appropriate policy responses.

Saving Biological Diversity: Economic Incentives identifies absent markets, insufficient price signals and misguided government policies (perverse subsidies and development policies) as the most prevalent underlying causes of biodiversity loss and concentrates on correcting these through the assignment of property rights and the correction of price signals through the removal of adverse subsidies and the incorporation of estimated biodiversity values. Significantly, it also focuses on the problems of uncertainty and information failure which lead to the non-reflection of the value of biological diversity in market prices.

With respect to policy design, it emphasised for the first time the need to apply a mix of measures – combining information and education with regulation and institution-building as well as with economic incentives proper such as environmental charges, subsidies or the assignment of well-defined property rights. This emphasis on a mix of measures foreshadowed the presentations and results of the OECD International Conference on Incentive Measures for the Conservation and the Sustainable Use of Biological Diversity in Cairns, Australia, 25-28 March 1996, and published subsequently as *Investing in Biological Diversity: The Cairns Conference* (OECD, 1997b). Many of the presentations indeed emphasised the unique character of biological diversity as an inherently complex and dynamically evolving system in whose regard uncertainty and ignorance are not so much failures which should be overcome, but intrinsic elements of biodiversity and to some extent an indicator of its richness and inexhaustibility.[2]

Box III.3. Underlying causes of biodiversity loss and suggested policy responses

Underlying causes	Policy response
Market failures, including unsustainable patterns of production and consumption	Address externalities through economic incentives and regulations; remove barriers to markets for biodiversity products.
Information failures	Invest in the generation of bio-physical, economic and social information about biodiversity, its values and the causes of its loss; involve and inform stakeholders.
Awareness failures[3]	Invest in the dissemination of information about the impacts of biodiversity depletion.
Policy failures, for example the subsidisation of activities which exert pressure on biodiversity	Remove or reform adverse subsidies, including below-cost pricing of resource concessions and free infrastructure provision.
Open access and dissipation of natural resource rents	Establish and clearly define property and use rights which allow rent capture and long-term planning.

Source: Adapted from OECD (1996).

Because of these uncertainties and informational failures, successful policies were found to be characterised by the *precautionary principle* and the idea of *safe minimum standards* to prevent major irreversibilities rather than by achieving an ideal of static optimisation. The message that only combinations of instruments formulated with a wide involvement of stakeholders and applied under specifically designed institutions with attention to the context of implementation could deliver successful results was strongly re-enforced. This highlighted questions of information provision and education, as well as distributional impacts of new incentive measures, monitoring and enforcement.

Both previous reports are at the source of the approach pursued throughout the *Handbook* of utilising a combination of market and non-market incentives. As

---

explained in more detail below, the main policy challenge in the field of biological diversity consists in managing the interaction between private activities with clear costs and rewards and the conservation of ecosystems which contain the elements of biological diversity but whose boundaries are fuzzy, whose values are ill-defined and often barely definable, but which in their entirety are essential parts of the framework which guarantees quality of life, the ability for economic production and ultimately the habitability of the earth.[4]

3. Outlook on future work

The work undertaken by the OECD Expert Group on the Economic Aspects of Biodiversity, including the production of this Handbook, will feed into the priorities for new work that were discussed at the Fourth Annual Meeting of the Conference of Parties to the Convention on Biological Diversity in Bratislava, 4-15 May 1998. In particular, Article IV/10A of the Decisions adopted by the Conference of Parties stressed the link between the assessment of biodiversity and the implementation of appropriate incentive measures:

> Recognizing that economic valuation of biodiversity and biological resources is an important tool for well-targeted and calibrated economic incentive measures,
>
> 1. Encourage Parties, Governments and relevant organizations:
>
>   a) To promote the design and implementation of appropriate incentive measures, taking fully into account the ecosystem approach and the various conditions of the Parties and employing the precautionary approach...;
>
>   ...
>
>   c) To take into account economic, social, cultural and ethical valuation in the development of relevant incentive measures;
>
>   ...

The same decision requests the Executive Secretary of the Convention on Biological Diversity

> b) To prepare in collaboration with the Organisation for Economic Development and Co-operation (OECD), the World Conservation Union (IUCN) and other relevant organizations, a background paper containing further analysis of the design and implementation of incentive measures for the conservation and sustainable use of biodiversity... with the aim of developing guidance to parties;
>
> c) To describe, in this document, ways and means to identify perverse incentives and possibilities to remove or mitigate their negative effects on biological diversity.

The OECD Expert Group on the Economic Aspects of Biodiversity and the Secretariat will work in the context of its mandate and the overall OECD work on sustainable development on both aspects. The assessment and the evaluation of biodiversity and biological resources, with an emphasis on the productive services of ecosystems, is the focus of the proposed new mandate of the (renamed) Working Group on Economic Aspects of Biodiversity. At the same time, the mandate includes the preparation of a background paper on incentive measures. In both cases, this *Handbook* will be the basis from which these future efforts will proceed.

OECD 1999

IV. The Multiple Values of Biodiversity and their Implications

Due to the multi-dimensionality of biodiversity, its conservation and sustainable use poses challenges to the policy-maker which differ from those in other areas of environmental policy making such as, for instance, environmental pollution. When tackling vehicle emissions in densely populated areas, for example, both the causes – emissions of nitrogen oxide and the creation of photogenic ozone – and the detrimental impacts on human well-being – irritation, increased morbidity – are fairly well known.

This knowledge of impacts and causes, and perhaps even of their respective monetary costs and benefits, allows policy-makers to proceed towards the internalisation of the external effects created by vehicle emissions through the application of economic instruments or regulations. These may include taxes on emissions or on inputs strictly related to emissions such as fuels, or regulations such as a requirement to use catalytic converters. Ideally, private costs and the public benefits from more sustainable behaviour will be balanced in the process, and overall welfare will be increased through the correction of a market failure.

The case of biodiversity is different. The causes affecting biodiversity and, even more so their impacts, are more complex and are rarely known with any precision. The term "biodiversity" refers to the intrinsic indivisibility of ecological phenomena. This leads to difficulties in information and the measurement of preferences in the formulation of economic incentive measures. In practice, it is rarely possible to identify a *single* proximate cause or a *single* underlying cause for the loss of biodiversity, as many of the chosen categories have unavoidable links with each other. Due to the complex nature of biodiversity, the underlying causes may not even be clearly identifiable. Box IV.1 provides a summary of some of the complexities facing biodiversity policy.

The complexity of biodiversity implies that a large number of actors affect biodiversity, as well as are affected by its existence or loss. The conservation and sustainable use of biodiversity are thus the concern of conservationists, entrepreneurs, local populations, and policy-makers – with their range of different objec-

---

Box IV.1. The challenges of biodiversity policy

- **Heterogeneity:** lack of homogeneity due to overlapping ecosystems, interdependent ecological functions and millions of species.

- **Irreversibility:** frequently, once past a certain threshold, impacts are irreversible as in the case of species extinction or ecosystem collapse; appropriate policies can thus not always balance present private and public costs, but should adhere to the precautionary principle.

- **Accumulation of impacts:** impacts accumulate and can create large losses in the long-run, while potentially smaller costs of prevention have to be incurred in the immediate present.

- **Information gaps:** the inherent complexity of ecosystems, as well as a general lack of information, require policy-makers to take decisions under uncertainty.

- **Mix of values:** biodiversity provides *private* use values; local, regional and global ecosystem services; and *public* existence values – this complicates the co-ordination of stakeholders.

- **Mix of pressures:** there are a mix of pressures on biodiversity which arise from different economic sectors due to a complex web of underlying causes.

- **Trans-national aspect:** the pressures on biodiversity, the resulting impacts, and the appropriate solutions often cross geo-political boundaries and require multi-lateral co-operation.

Source: Adapted from Young and Gunningham (1997).

---

tives. This large number of stakeholders complicates the assessment of the benefits of biodiversity conservation. In addition, there are practical problems of implementing conservation measures linked to questions of political economy such as distribution, stakeholder involvement, monitoring and enforcement. The case studies, however, indicate that some promising approaches exist for tackling these issues and simultaneously realising the multiple values of biodiversity.

A final characteristic which distinguishes problems of biodiversity depletion from classical pollution problems is that the former are often accompanied by a policy vacuum. Due to open access and ill-defined property rights, often not even all the private use benefits of biodiversity can be captured, so both private users and the general public sustain heavy losses from its depletion. As has been frequently stated in the literature, such a situation leads to great economic inefficiencies. Unregulated open access of a valuable resource will lead to its inefficient use on a first-come, first-serve basis with rapid depletion as a necessary consequence.[5]

The complexities surrounding biodiversity translate from the sphere of assessment and instrument design into the sphere of implementation. Coalition building is difficult as the benefits of biodiversity are spread over a large number of people, while the costs of its conservation are likely to be borne by a much smaller, more cohesive group of people which will be able to wield more effective influence in policy-making terms. Similarly, monitoring and enforcement of incentive measures are made more difficult by the large number of actors and indicators. The formidable difficulties facing policy-makers in the definition even of policy objectives for the conservation of biodiversity are highlighted by the example in Box IV.2 concerning such a seemingly straightforward example as the definition of a "species".

In the face of such difficulties, to even define the basic objectives of incentive measures for the conservation and the sustainable use of biodiversity, policy design has to take a step backwards. The first stage in the design and implementation of incentive measures for the conservation and the sustainable use of biodiversity has to be the characterisation of its intrinsic values. On this basis, objectives can be discussed and incentive measures developed. The next sub-chapter presents the main dimensions of the value components of biological diversity.

I. The multiple values of biodiversity

Regardless of how biodiversity is defined (see Box IV.2), it necessarily comprises a vast amount of organisms and habitats and their interactions. 'Complexity' – the property of a system which indicates that the total relations between the elements of the system are not exhausted by the sum of the relations of each single element – is the hallmark of biological diversity.

For the economist this poses the challenge of translating this complexity, and its value in terms of human well-being, into categories which are simple and tangible enough to be communicable to stakeholders and policy decision-makers. From the point of view of economic theory, all values of biodiversity, as well as all the values of its elements, would ideally be translatable into monetary terms. Unfortunately, even in the best cases, such monetisation is often only an approximation (see p. 107). In order to strengthen biodiversity policies, it is important that the available techniques for determining economic valuations of its benefits are further developed and utilised wherever possible. Fortunately, while monetisation is desirable if it is able to express widely held and appropriately defined appreciation of elements of biodiversity, appropriate policies can usually still be formulated using only implicit values for these aspects.

Whether economic values for biodiversity goods and services can be estimated or not, a clear definition and understanding of the different values of biodiversity is essential. Box IV.3 provides a first overview of the different categories

OECD 1999

Box IV.2. What is biodiversity?

According to the Convention on Biological Diversity, "*biological diversity* means the variability among living organisms from all sources including, *inter alia*, terrestrial, marine and other aquatic ecosystems and the ecological complexes of which they are part; this includes diversity within species, between species and of ecosystems" (UNEP, 1994). The term 'biodiversity' thus refers to the variety of all life on earth, and explicitly recognises how the interaction of the different components of ecosystems result in the provision of essential ecosystem services on the one hand, and social and recreational opportunities on the other, including being a source of inspiration and cultural identity (Commonwealth of Australia, 1996).

A number of concepts have been developed in recent years relating to indicators of or principles for biodiversity management, including "ecosystem integrity", "ecosystem health", "sustainability", and "resilience" (the ability of an ecosystem to withstand stresses and shocks). The variety of concepts and definitions that abound indicates the difficulties facing any attempts to establish a practical, working definition of biological diversity. Perhaps one of the simplest and most widely-accepted definitions used is the conservation of the maximum number of species. But even here there are difficulties as it is not clear what actually constitutes a species. Some common concepts for differentiating species have been identified by Brookes (1998) as:

- *biological species concept* – defines a species as a group of interbreeding populations isolated from other such groups;
- *morphological species definition* – defines a species according to a given set of common features;
- *evolutionary species concept* – defines a species by its shared evolutionary history; and
- *genotypic cluster definition* – uses genetic "gaps" to distinguish between species.

Each of these definitions tries to isolate a species out from the wider concepts of ecosystem and biodiversity, but the variety of definitions in use indicates the difficulties inherent in such an exercise.

---

developed by economic theory of the values of biodiversity. While it is not part of the scope of this *Handbook* to discuss the derivation of these values, it is helpful to outline their nature and, in particular, to highlight the fact that they require different incentive measures for their realisation.[6]

Direct use values: use value is concerned with those elements of biodiversity which can be directly consumed, traded or used as an input to commercial activities. Examples include plants or animals that are collected or hunted for nutrition, clothing or housing. Often elements of biodiversity are exported to realise their use value, for instance, exotic hardwoods, ornamental fish, exotic birds, hides, ivory tusks etc. Use values can usually be realised by individuals (or companies) and are hence *privately appropriable*. This can include the use of certain areas or ecosystems for activities such as sight-seeing or tourism (amenity value).

Direct use values can generally be estimated by looking at the market prices for specific products or close substitutes. Use values are least likely to be successfully realised in situations where property or use rights are unclear, such that the intrinsic value of the resources can be rapidly dissipated through hasty short-term exploitation or sub-optimal uses, *e.g.* unlicensed timber-harvesting or slash-and-burn agriculture. An important incentive measure for the realisation of use values is the allocation of well-defined property rights in connection with the provision of information about long-run impacts (see p. 79). Tradable property rights can eventually lead to the emergence of markets, providing transaction costs are not too high.

Indirect use values or ecosystem services: ecosystem services are all those functions of the environment which provide direct value to the well-being of humans whether on a local, regional or global level through the maintenance of a healthy natural environment. This can include flood control or the prevention of soil erosion on a local level, the purification of water supplies at the regional level, or carbon sequestration and the stabilisation of the oxygen supply at a global level. The value of ecosystem services, or rather their lower bound, can frequently be assessed by calculating the amount which is necessary to invest in installations or technologies to substitute for them, *e.g.* the price of an equivalent water purification plant could be a proxy for the value of an ecosystem assuring water quality.[7]

Incentive measures for the sustainable use of ecosystems and the conservation of their services can reach from fiscal instruments such as emission taxes which limit the pressures on ecosystems to institutional mechanisms for the assessment of the total amount of services provided and least-cost options for their maintenance. Contrary to the realisation of direct use values, however, the realisation of ecosystem services requires a social or public dimension, as the benefits of ecosystems are not privately appropriable.

Option and quasi-option value: option values and quasi-option values represent the value which is contained in having the ability to make choices in an uncertain future. Option values concern choices which people would like to be able to make if their preferences change. For example, one might not attach any present (nor even perhaps any future) direct or indirect use value to a given ecosystem, but one might attach value to the possibility of using the ecosystem in case one's preferences change. Quasi-option values concern maintaining the ability to react to future information (it is occasionally also referred to as the expected value of future informa-

29

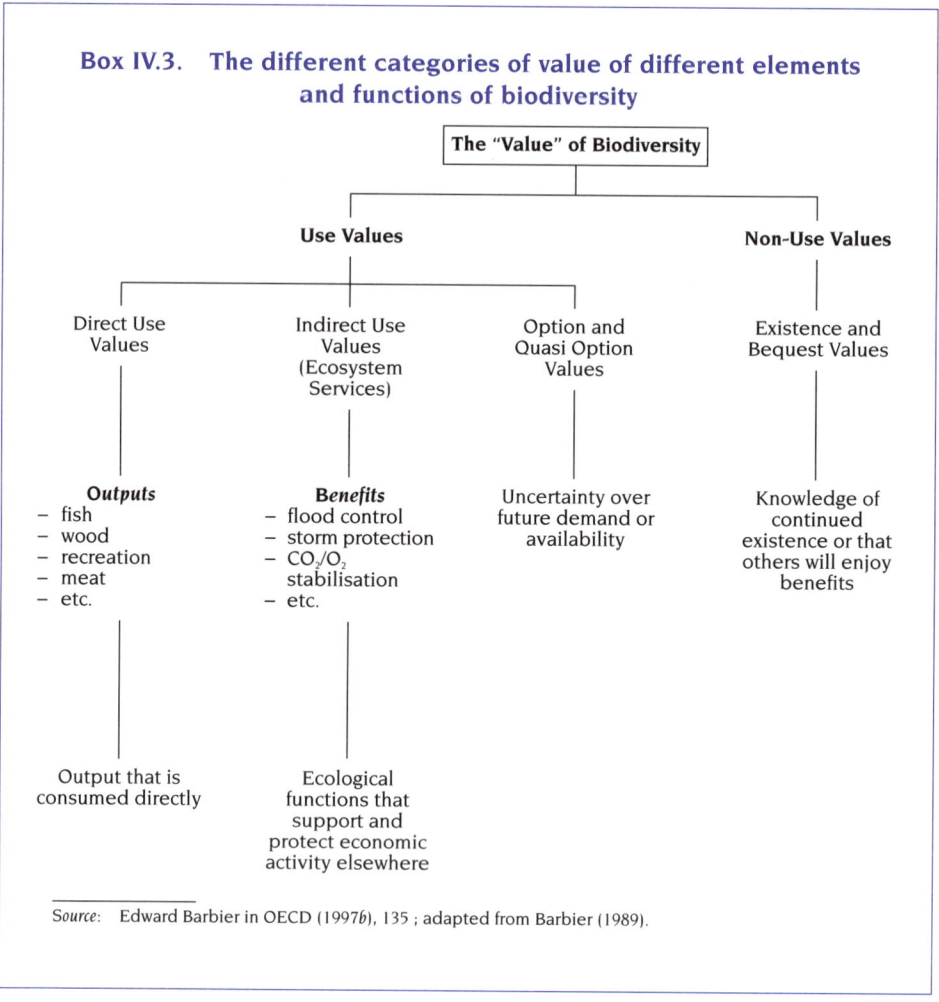

Box IV.3. The different categories of value of different elements and functions of biodiversity

Source: Edward Barbier in OECD (1997b), 135 ; adapted from Barbier (1989).

tion) independently of one's own current preferences and knowledge. For example, the stratospheric ozone layer had no known use value before the discovery of its capability to absorb UV-radiation. However, it already contained a quasi-option value due to the possibility that it *might* have some, as of then unknown, uses.

Since option and quasi-option values can concern essentially all direct and indirect use values of biological diversity, specific incentive measures for their realisation are not common. Benefit sharing arrangements for genetic resources is one example of a measure which can help to capture the option value of these resources. A series of general considerations can also be applied to ensure the capture of *potential* future use values: applying the *precautionary principle* in general policy-making expresses a will to preserve option and quasi-option values; likewise, all policies which enhance the range of possible future actions, whether through the conservation of ranges of ecosystems, increased flexibility or decentralised decision-making to spread risks, contribute to the realisation and enhancement of option values.

Existence or bequest values: existence values refer to the fact that humans value ecosystems and biological diversity for their pure existence, and bequest values for the possibility of maintaining them for future generations. The knowledge that tropical rain forests, the whale or the Panda bear continue to exist provides satisfaction to people even if they might never do so much as to look at a picture of one. Existence values are closely linked to cultural, or even religious, values and form part of our general conceptions of nature. Perceptions of existence values are socially established, and these values frequently increase with income levels.

Attempts to realise existence values have often involved transfers (subsidies) from those groups experiencing the existence values to those groups who are required to realise them through the privately costly adoption of sustainable use practices.[8] In the case of global biodiversity, existence values are frequently experienced, and partly financed, by people in comparatively wealthy Northern countries, whereas the recipients of transfers are frequently found in biodiversity-rich Southern countries. These transfers are organised through bi-lateral grants or grants to international non-governmental organisations, such as the Global Environment Facility.[9] Environmental Funds (see p. 94) are also an efficient way of realising existence values. In practice, transfers of funds for the maintenance of existence values are often closely linked to, and frequently indistinguishable from, payments for the use value associated with aesthetic enjoyment or payments for the provision of global ecosystem services such as carbon sequestration.

The incentive measures needed to conserve and enhance biological diversity are as varied as the values embodied in this diversity. In the vast majority of cases, each species, ecosystem and element of it contains a combination of use, option and existence values. It is thus not surprising that incentive measures implemented for the conservation and the sustainable use of biodiversity frequently have to fulfil more than one objective and are often most effective when used in combination with each other. The twenty-two case studies provided by Member countries show a rich variety of incentive measures and their combinations. Chapter VII presents a synthesis of the experiences with the incentive measures used in these case studies, and Annex II gives an overview of each case study.

OECD 1999

2. Incentive measures to realise the private and the public values of biodiversity

The greatest policy challenge in the implementation of incentive measures is the fact that biodiversity extends to the private as well as to the public sphere and that incentive measures have to take both aspects into account. Private benefits are those that can be appropriated by single economic actors, individuals or companies. They result from goods (such as a genetic resource) or services (such as an amenity like a scenic view) that are provided by biodiversity and that can be traded in a market. Private benefits are thus usually measurable in monetary terms and correspond to the 'direct use values' discussed above. The appropriate policy response to realise the private value of biodiversity is to establish and enforce well-defined property rights over clearly-defined resources.

Assuming that the distributional intricacies of property rights allocations can be resolved, the allocation of well-defined property and use rights can induce the owners of these rights to maximise the net present value of all future benefit streams stemming from their resources. Assuming competitive markets, trading will assure that the owners who can realise the most benefits from the resources, and so who are able to pay the highest price for them, will eventually own and harvest the resources. The provision of well-defined property rights is a significant improvement over the inefficiencies associated with unregulated open-access.

Private owners, however, will usually pay attention to only those values which they can reap, in other words, those values which are privately appropriable.[10] Many aspects of biological diversity, however, such as its public existence values, cannot be privately appropriated and hence are not reflected in the decisions of private owners. Other than in those cases in which these values are intrinsically linked to some private benefits, they are generally thus disregarded. These public goods and services of biodiversity do not accrue to any single economic actor, but to society at large, whether at the global, regional, national or even at the local level. Since biodiversity as a whole is characterised by very high complexity and by numerous linkages between its individual components, almost all elements of biodiversity contributes to these public existence values to the extent that it contributes to the functioning of the whole of biological diversity and life supporting systems.

An adjustment in behaviour in order to realise the existence values of biodiversity as well, for example through a switch from unsustainable to sustainable logging, would bring public benefits, but would also create costs in terms of private losses. Without additional policies to close this profitability gap, these existence values will generally not be realised by the allocation of property rights alone. Policies for the optimisation of public good values can include direct transfers and the implementation of all those instruments that *conserve* biodiversity. A classic example is the establishment of a natural park where use of biodiversity is restricted to non-consumptive activities such as sight-seeing. However, any kind of regulation or covenant that restricts the use of biodiversity and limits activities that might exert pressure on it is a policy instrument to conserve the public value of biodiversity.

Of course, this should not imply that private use can *never* realise public benefits by itself. For instance, agricultural production can have aesthetic and rural amenity values and so can contribute to these uncompensated positive externalities.[11] Similarly, the privately sustainable use of commercial fisheries realises their public existence values as well as their private (Gudmundsson *et al.*, 1997).

In fact, one reason for the tension between private and public values is often *information failure*, such that when private owners are furnished with more or better information, they are more able to take into consideration the long-term impacts of their actions. Equally, the public sector can better target any incentive measures it uses when there is precise information available about the adverse impacts of the private activities to be addressed. As a result, as will be discussed further in the section on "Economic valuation as incentive measure and support for decision-making" below, the revelation of the value of biodiversity can act as an incentive for its conservation. Individuals, stakeholders, decision makers, etc. are often unaware of how significant these values are, so that revealing them can lead to an improved awareness of the importance of biodiversity to the well-being of society as a whole. The measurement of the public economic values of biodiversity which are not self-evident can help to overcome information failures and allow decisions about the use of biological resources to better consider all of their values.

Thus, contributions to the public values associated with biodiversity *can* be forthcoming from private use of the resources. Policies for the conservation and the sustainable use of biodiversity have to assure that they are forthcoming in every case and that both the private and public values of biodiversity are thus fully realised.

3. Conservation, sustainable use and benefit sharing in the Convention on Biological Diversity

International work on the sustainable use of biodiversity necessarily takes place in the context of the Convention on Biological Diversity and the other biodiversity-related conventions.[12] The case studies as well as this *Handbook* are understood as contributions to the implementation of the Convention. The Convention on Biological Diversity states as its three objectives the conservation of biological diversity, the sustainable use of its components, and the fair and equitable sharing of the benefits arising out of the utilisation of genetic resources. All three stress different aspects of the biodiversity issue. The careful consideration of all three objectives is necessary for the design and implementation of successful incentive measures. For this Handbook and the case studies to contribute to the implementation of the Convention, the role that incentive measures are to play in achieving these objectives must be clearly understood.

Box IV.4. Article 1 of the Convention on Biological Diversity: objectives

"The objectives of this Convention to be pursued in accordance with its relevant provisions, are the conservation of biodiversity, the sustainable use of its components and the fair and equitable sharing of the benefits arising out of the utilisation of genetic resources, including by appropriate access to genetic resources and by appropriate transfer of relevant technologies, taking into account all rights over those resources and to technologies, and by appropriate funding."

Conservation: The conservation of biological diversity can be understood as the implementation of measures to ensure that biological resources and their ecosystems or habitats are maintained such that there is the absence of a decline in biodiversity. While biodiversity consists of the three components of genetic, species and ecosystem biodiversity, it is the conservation of ecosystems and consequently the conservation of species and genetic resources *in situ* which is accorded special status under the Convention on Biological Diversity (Article 8). *In situ* conservation can be complemented by the promotion of *ex situ* conservation where appropriate (Article 9). Conservation under the Convention is not so much understood as an attempt to protect any particular *status quo* in museum-like perfection, but rather to conserve and enhance the ability of ecosystems to develop and re-generate themselves as living systems. While certain areas of particular value, or biodiversity "hotspots" might be in special need of protection by means of access restrictions, the notion of conservation is usually understood as the absence of a decline of biodiversity.

Sustainable use: The term "sustainable use" receives a precise definition in Article 2 of the Convention where it is defined as "... the use of components of biological diversity in a way and at a rate that does not lead to the long-term decline of biological diversity, thereby maintaining its potential to meet the needs and aspirations of present and future generations". The notion of sustainable use complements and supports the notion of conservation. It refers to activities which are privately profitable but contribute *at the same time* to the conservation of biological diversity. As such, it implies the meeting of the private goals and needs of individuals and stakeholders – including the social, livelihood, aesthetic, ethical and potential use values – as well as the public goals of conservation.

. OECD 1999

Sustainable use is one of the key elements of the Convention, and the most important for consideration in this *Handbook*. Rightfully, it has therefore received a very high degree of attention in the case studies provided by OECD Member countries. As an activity which is undertaken for private profit, sustainable use responds to price signals like any other economic activity. However, sustainable use is distinguished from other economic activities by the fact that it is expected to contribute to the *public good* aspect of biodiversity conservation as well. Therefore, individuals or companies who pursue sustainable use of the components of biological diversity are expected to abstain from the (often more profitable in the short-term) *unsustainable use* of biodiversity.

Given the differential in profitability that often exists, private entrepreneurs would have a tendency to choose unsustainable use in the absence of additional incentive measures. Incentive measures are thus needed to bridge the profitability gap between sustainable and unsustainable use. Realising the public goods aspects of biodiversity (where these do not already coincide with realising the private values) generally has to be paid for either in terms of reduced private profits or through government budget transfers.[13] Where sustainable use is privately profitable (for example, as for some eco-tourism activities), and biodiversity is adequately protected, a policy problem does not exist. Policies and incentive measures are thus required only where the private and public values do not coincide.

An additional difficulty that is raised in connection with sustainable use is reaching agreement on an exact definition of the criteria for "sustainability". For instance, activities which are perfectly sustainable on a small or medium scale might be unsustainable on a larger scale. Some types of tourism or flora or fauna harvesting might provide very promising forms of sustainable use, while others might not. In practice, conflict between almost any use of biological resources and conservation objectives can arise. Embracing the policy goal of "sustainable use" is to accept the challenge of this tension and to manage it in an even-handed way. Clear criteria which concretely define sustainable practices can assist the implementation of this policy goal.

The concept of sustainable use of biological resources is also closely related to one of the overall aims of the OECD: to achieve policy integration between environmental and economic objectives. As such, working towards the sustainable use of biological resources and ecosystems amounts to encouraging economic development and environmental protection goals that are mutually compatible, rather than conflicting.

Benefit sharing: The third objective of the Convention on Biological Diversity is perhaps the most difficult one from the point of view of policy development. While all three objectives set forward challenges in combining private and public considerations, the complexities involved in achieving a "fair sharing of benefits arising from the utilisation of genetic resources" are perhaps the most intricate. This is due to the number of different groups of actors involved (with each group having its own aspirations and agenda), and the uncertainties of the quantitative estimates of the benefits of conservation or sustainable use as well as of the relative contributions each group of actors should or is making to the realisation of the benefits. Benefit sharing is often seen in a so-called North-versus-South perspective, with industrialised countries (the North) as the users of genetic resources, while developing countries (the South) are the suppliers. However, the sharing of the benefits of biodiversity can also take place between countries in either group, as well as within any country.

Benefit sharing can work very much as an incentive measure for the sustainable use of a particular component of biodiversity, *i.e.*, genetic resources. However, issues of capacity building and technology sharing, trade and intellectual property rights, make it an issue for other fora and discussions. In this *Handbook*, incentive measures for the sustainable use of genetic resources are not explicitly excluded, but the focus is certainly on other components of biodiversity, such as species and ecosystems.[14]

4. The need for combinations of instruments

Almost all benefits associated with biodiversity have private as well as public aspects. A rare scenic view can be used by an eco-tourism enterprise and its customers but also contains an existence value beyond the immediate users. The implication for policy makers is straightforward: instruments have to be implemented that address both the private and public aspects of biodiversity. Successful policies for the conservation and the sustainable use of biodiversity thus have to use instruments which not only protect direct use values through the provision of well-defined property rights, but also its public values, perhaps through additional instruments such as positive incentives or regulations which guarantee the compatibility of use with the conservation of biodiversity. As a result, successful approaches in most cases require *combinations of incentives*.

Applying a combination of incentive measures can also help to overcome the other challenges that face biodiversity policy, such as those that are listed in Box IV.1. By using a range of instruments targeted to different pressures, there is a greater likelihood that all the underlying causes of biodiversity loss will be addressed, thus reducing the likelihood of causing irreversible damage. Again, given the uncertainties and information gaps that surround biodiversity policy making, and the pressures that serve to deplete biodiversity, a mix of incentives can be useful even when there is only one source of biodiversity loss to address (see Chapter VII).

> ## Box IV.5. Incentive measures to encourage the sustainable use and conservation of biodiversity
>
> - *Economic incentives*
>   - fees, charges and environmental taxes
>   - market creation and assignment of well-defined property rights
>   - reform or removal of adverse subsidies
> - *Regulations and funds*
>   - standards, regulations and access restrictions
>   - environmental funds and public financing
> - *Framework incentives*
>   - information provision, scientific and technical capacity building
>   - economic valuation
>   - institution building and stakeholder involvement

There are a number of examples of successful combinations of incentives for biodiversity conservation or sustainable use, including the granting of well-defined property rights linked to either covenants specifying the allowable uses of the resources, the granting of tax advantages for certain activities, or even the use of agri-environmental payments for agricultural practices that contribute to the maintenance of species and ecosystems (see Box IV.6 and Section VII.4 for further examples). All these incentives ensure that the private profitability gap between sustainable and unsustainable use of the biological resources is closed. Private users of the elements of biodiversity are either under the obligation – in return for the ability to extract use values from them – to contribute to public values through sustainable use, or are compensated for doing so.[15]

Such a strategy could be called "markets plus". It is essentially based on hybrid instruments that combine economic incentives for private actors with a conditionality that ensures a contribution to the public good of biodiversity conservation. Depending on the specific arrangements concerning property rights in different societies, such incentives can be positive, *e.g.* a subsidy or a property right, or negative, *e.g.* a tax or an access restriction. It is not the type of instrument used that is important at this point, but the fact that whichever instrument is chosen has to conform to the exigencies of sustainable use, *i.e.* a use that is privately profitable to the largest possible extent while still contributing fully to the conservation of biodiversity.

OECD 1999

Box IV.6. Combinations of instruments to realise the public *and* private values of biodiversity

- Well-defined property rights are combined with covenants, obligations, conditions, management agreements, agri-environmental measures, etc.;

- Property rights over natural resources are substituted by *use rights* which can ensure highest return from direct use values while covering only certain aspects or requiring conditionality of use (*e.g.*, tradable development rights, certification); and

- Market creation for private uses with positive spill-overs through sustainable use (*e.g.* sustainable agriculture) can be encouraged through information provision and the covering of incremental costs.

Since its beginnings, the OECD Expert Group on Economic Aspects of Biodiversity has been associated with an emphasis on economic incentives, as was also reflected in the title of its first major publication, *Saving Biological Diversity: Economic Incentives* (1996). This perspective of 'getting the prices right' has been dominant throughout the work of the Group and has encompassed both the introduction of positive, environmentally-beneficial incentives, such as the use of environmental funds or fiscal incentives for conservation activities, and the removal of adverse incentives by internalising the costs of biodiversity loss through charges and taxes, and reducing support to activities which exert pressure on biological diversity.

Competitive markets are generally the most efficient allocation mechanism for privately appropriable goods, including many of the individual components of biodiversity. At the same time, the assignment of well-defined property rights over land or certain biodiversity resources can overcome uncertainty and provide a long-term incentive for enhancing the overall value of the resource. But implementing 'the right prices' and establishing well-defined property rights can only successfully prevent biodiversity loss if markets are able to transmit the appropriate values of biodiversity in their entirety. Unfortunately, many aspects of biodiversity will not be adequately conserved through markets, as they are too complex and too diffuse to be privately allocated. For example, it is unlikely that there currently exists any market in which the tropical rain forest would receive its full value.

Thus, while market-based instruments will often be the most cost-effective and efficient incentives to encourage the sustainable use of biological resources, in many cases it will be necessary to also use regulations and restrictions in order to ensure the appropriate level of conservation. The Expert Group on Economic

Aspects of Biodiversity has thus proceeded in a perspective of well-defined property and use rights and economic incentives such as environmental charges wherever possible, and regulations, access restrictions and subsidisation of sustainable use wherever necessary. In addition, stakeholder involvement, capacity and institution building, and information provision have been recognised as important complements to both categories of instruments. This approach of "markets plus" combines the allocation of property rights with a certain conditionality of their use, thus advocating the use of hybrid instruments which both realise the private good aspect of many components of biodiversity and their intrinsic public good aspect.

OECD 1999

V.   Different Ecosystems – Different Challenges

The Conference of the Parties to the Convention on Biological Diversity has emphasised repeatedly that it wishes to pursue its work in the context of an eco-system approach (see Box V.1). Ecosystems are functional units of biodiversity and its elements which can (and often do) overlap. Each ecosystem has its own char-acteristics – geographically, biologically and in terms of its resilience to different types of pressures resulting from human activities. By emphasising an ecosystem approach, the Conference of the Parties highlights that each of these functional units has its own specific characteristics and requires incentive measures which are suited to its particular needs. For example, a sparsely-populated but fragile moun-tain area will require a different set of incentive measures than an inland freshwater ecosystem subject to population and land-use pressures.

Box V.1.   The ecosystem approach to biodiversity conservation

Ecosystems are the dynamic network of biological, chemical, and physical inter-actions that sustain a community and allow it to respond to changes in environmental conditions. The size of an ecosystem is not fixed, but is defined in terms of the systems that are under study.

The second meeting of SBSTTA[16] indicated the importance of approaching biodi-versity conservation through the examination of whole ecosystems, rather than focus-ing on individual components within them. The importance of this "ecosystem approach" was underscored in the third meeting of the Conference of the Parties to the Convention on Biological Diversity in Buenos Aires, 4-15 November 1996.

So far, the following thematic areas have been considered by the Conference of the Parties: marine and coastal, agricultural, forest and inland water biological diver-sity. While these "themes" are not directly equivalent to ecosystems, they have all been considered in the ecosystem approach (UNEP/CBD/COP/4/Inf.9). Other terrestrial areas – including dryland, Mediterranean, and mountain ecosystems – will be consid-ered under the future work programme.

Of course, the applicability of incentive measures not only varies with the eco-system, but also with respect to the sector or constituency at which it is targeted. The response of the relevant actors to different incentive measures depends on the nature of the stakeholders involved and their political, legal and social standing. Thus, for example, different incentive measures will be effective for encouraging illegal game poachers to cease these activities (perhaps regulations with sufficient enforcement, or legalisation and market creation) than may be appropriate for encouraging farmers to alter their farming techniques to encourage biodiversity (perhaps more educational provision and co-operative decision-making, including the use of compensatory payments).

As a result, many pressures on biodiversity arise from economic activities that cut across several ecosystems. These cross-cutting pressures might be best addressed by specific types of incentive measures implemented at a sectoral level instead of at the ecosystem level.

Ecosystems and economic sectors interact with different degrees of intensity. The framework according to which the country case studies were prepared (OECD, 1997*a*) presented a first indicative overview of the interactions between ecosys-tems and sectors which is reproduced in Box V.2 below. The strength of impact of the pressures on biodiversity, of course, varies between different sectors and eco-systems in different countries. The box thus provides only a qualitative indication of "significant impacts".

The rest of this Chapter discusses the specific problems faced by the major ecosystems described in the case studies and the most important human activities which influence – either positively or negatively – the conservation and the sus-tainable use of biodiversity in these ecosystems. The particular pressures on the different ecosystems are discussed, as well as both their proximate (direct) and their underlying causes, as identified in the twenty-two case studies provided by Member countries.

A cross-cutting issue faced by all ecosystems is species loss. If the number of known plant and animal species that are "endangered" or "vulnerable" are taken as an indicator for the ecological status of biodiversity, one can see that on average 3 per cent of known species for which enough data is available in OECD countries are considered endangered or vulnerable (OECD, 1997*d*).[17] For mammals and amphibians, this ratio is much higher, at 23 and 22 per cent respectively. However, for invertebrates, which constitute the largest genus of known animals, the per-centage of known species that are endangered or vulnerable is just under 3 per cent. These figures only provide averages across a number of OECD countries. Of course, significant variations in the number of species and the nature of threats exist between countries.

Box V.2. Indicative overview of interactions between ecosystems and economic sectors

Ecosystems →

Sectoral Pressures↓	Coastal Zones	Marine Eco-systems	Arable Land	Forests	Inland freshwater ecosystems	Mountn. and Subm. Regions	Grass- and Range-lands	Arid- and Semiarid Areas
Tourism	*	*		*	*	*	*	*
Fishery	*	*			*			
Road Transport	*		*	*	*	*	*	*
Agriculture	*		*	*	*	*	*	*
Forestry			*	*	*	*		
Land-use	*		*	*	*	*	*	*
Shipping	*	*						
Industry	*		*	*	*			*

Unfortunately, the available data suggests that in many countries substantial proportions of the species that are known to exist were continuing to decrease in numbers during the mid-1990s. This is particularly true for amphibians and reptiles. Thus, over 25 per cent of the populations of known amphibians in OECD countries are decreasing, with all of the known amphibious species in New Zealand, Hungary, Luxembourg and Poland decreasing (OECD, 1998b).

1. Marine ecosystems and coastal zones

Marine ecosystems and coastal zones are, of course, closely linked in that they are both affected by the same environmental medium, the global oceans, which cover almost three-quarters of the world's surface. While commercial fisheries constitute an important sector affecting *marine ecosystems*, they are but one of a number of pressures bearing on these biodiversity-rich areas. Other pressures include industrial pollution, tourism, aquaculture, etc. In terms of *coastal zones*, however, it is tourism that creates in many cases the most intense pressures in OECD countries, especially in European countries. But these zones are also subject to a range of other pressures, being amongst the most densely populated and most heavily exploited ecosystems in OECD countries and possibly world-wide.

Marine ecosystems and fisheries

Marine ecosystems are one of the last remaining global commons. While marine ecosystems are generally fairly biodiversity rich, this varies considerably by area, with coastal waters being particularly biodiverse. The open sea, by contrast, contains 90 per cent of the world's ocean area, but only 10 per cent of ocean species.

Commercial fishing activities exert pressures on marine resources. The main pressures on commercial fish populations that arise from fishing activities include the negative effects of high-grading[18] and the harvesting of unsustainable levels of fish. Other non-target species and the surrounding ecosystem can also be damaged through the discarding of by-catch.

Box V.3. Facts about marine ecosystems

Characteristics: Fairly biodiverse, particularly near coastal zones. Species are often less endemic than land-based ones.

Size: Oceans cover over 70 per cent of the world's surface. Marine species account for 250 000 of the classified 1.7 million species in the world

Species loss: Over 70 per cent of the world stocks of marine fish were fully fished, over-fished, depleted or recovering in 1995. Stocks of commercial species are drastically declining. On average, almost 6 per cent of the known fish species in OECD countries are classified as "threatened".

Economic pressures: Primarily fisheries and maritime transport, although pollution from other sectors (such as agricultural run-off) also exerts pressures on marine ecosystems.

Sources: World Resources Institute (1996); OECD (1997c).

Other pressures come from, for example, the introduction of alien species, often through the dumping of ballast water from cargo ships; and the effect of pollution on the ecosystem, including the generation of toxic algae blooms and the release of toxic chemicals. Certain fishing methods, such as dynamite fishing, directly lead to the destruction of species' habitat. In the past, bottom trawling has also contributed to damages to the sea-bed. In certain Member countries, such as Japan, the problems are now being vigorously addressed and pressures on habitat from bottom trawling will be reduced.

There are also global environmental effects which impact on marine ecosystems, such as rising sea levels, increased UV-B exposure from depletion of the ozone layer and permanent changes in ocean temperatures as a result of climate change. Thus, in addition to the over-exploitation of some commercial fish species, the harvesting methods and levels currently practised in many OECD countries also have a more general, negative affect on marine biodiversity (Gudmundsson *et al.*, 1998). The underlying cause of these unsustainable production patterns results from an important economic failure: the lack of clearly defined property rights over these resources, as well as a lack of adequate control measures.

As will be seen below, fishing activities do lend themselves, in principle, to the creation of markets and the assignment of well-defined property rights, through, for example individual transferable quota systems (see Box VII.4). These quotas specify the amount of catch of a particular species the owner of the quota can harvest, thus allocating property rights over use of the species to the owners of the ITQs. Because the ITQ owners are assured of their right to harvest a certain quota of fish, they can utilise the most cost-effective harvesting methods, rather than having to engage in an inefficient and expensive race-to-fish. In addition, if the fishing quotas apply over a number of years, the owners will have an incentive to ensure harvests are sustainable such that future (profitable) fishing will be viable. As such, the ITQs provide incentives for long-term profit maximisation by the holders of the quotas, while ensuring the conservation of the privately valuable resources by allocating fishing quotas only up to a sustainable level.

While this reasoning is sound and incentive measures in this direction are being explored, an important caveat applies: the assignment of property rights over the exploitation of a given species – even in a long-term perspective – might well conserve the species, but might give little or no consideration to the surrounding ecosystem and its existence value. ITQs thus require the use of additional regulatory instruments in order to contribute effectively to the sustainable use of biodiversity. For example, to minimise the collateral damage that arises in the course of the exploitation of the privately valuable resource, additional incentives have to be provided in the form of licensing and effective regulations in order to assure the public existence value of the surrounding ecosystem and non-target species. Incentives for the wise use and management of ecosystems, education and capacity building, as well as the removal of subsidies which encourage unsustainable fishing and the imposition of environmental support measures (based on appropriate scientific evidence) also provide important measures for managing fisheries.

Thus, for fisheries management, ideally a combination of incentive measures will be used to encourage the sustainable use of the biological resources, including the assignment of property rights over the use of the commercially viable species, restrictions on the methods of fishing and the use of the surrounding ecosystem,

45

the removal or reform of subsidies which encourage unsustainable fishing activities, and capacity building and awareness raising.

Coastal zones and tourism

Coastal zones are one of the most heavily populated and most intensely used ecosystems on earth. With approximately 60 per cent of the world's human population living within 100 kilometres of the shore, there are intense pressures on these often fragile ecosystems (World Resources Institute, 1996). Fishery, tourism, shipping, agriculture, aquaculture, land-use, development, industry, and investment in infrastructure and public amenities place multiple pressures on biodiversity-rich and varied coastal ecosystems. The attractiveness of coastal zones and the competition for location and access makes the enforcement of sustainable use through the imposition of a network of regulations an important task.

Box V.4. Facts about coastal zones

Characteristics: Coastal zones include a number of ecosystems – such as estuaries, deltas, mangrove forests, and coastal wetlands.[19] They are highly biodiverse, but often fragile ecosystems. They are one of the most affected by human activities.

Size: Coastal zones hold nine-tenths of marine biodiversity. About 34 per cent of world's coasts are at high potential risk of degradation, and another 17 per cent at moderate risk.

Economic pressures: The main sectors affecting coastal zones are human settlement and tourism, coastal development and land-use, fisheries and aquaculture, shipping, and industrial pollution. The main pressures are habitat loss, intense over-exploitation, pollution and sedimentation, species introduction and climate change.

Source: World Resources Institute (1996).

The main proximate causes of biodiversity loss in coastal zones are habitat destruction and alteration, exploitation of wild species, and pollution. In addition, siltation and pollution of coastal waterways can lead to negative impacts in upstream catchments in terms of land degradation and pollution. The underlying causes are mainly the result of increasing demands from human consumption patterns (such as from tourism activities), population distribution pressures and various economic failures, including the lack of clearly defined property rights, information failure and the inadequacy of government intervention to address these threats through adequate planning and development strategies and regulations. Because coastal zones are often public lands that are threatened primarily by overuse of the zones themselves and incompatible use of surrounding private lands, regulations and access restrictions are the most common incentives applied for their protection or sustainable use.

One Member country case study emphasised the pressures brought to bear on coastal zones and islands from rapid tourism development during the 1970s and 1980s, in this case in Greece. The increasing numbers of visitors and the related amenities that were developed on the beach and at sea, sand compaction, beach litter, and the artificial noise and lights on the beach at night all led to significant pressure on the environment. In particular, the sand dune ecosystem and the endemic plants in the area under study were being destroyed and lost, and there were seasonal incidents of marine pollution from untreated wastes, which pose a direct threat to the nesting place of the endangered loggerhead sea turtle which was the focus of the study.

As with many other recently and rapidly developed tourist areas, many of the services described in this study do not maintain adequate safety and sanitary standards, with a lack of proper infrastructure particularly noticeable in the transportation network, the sewage collection system, the solid waste management system and the operation of marinas.

There are a range of regulations available to authorities for the protection of coastal zones, including building restrictions on the ecologically-sensitive lands and incentives for development elsewhere, restrictions on fishing and marine traffic, and visitor access and beach activity restrictions. Because of the difficulties of monitoring and enforcing regulations along the often extensive areas that comprise coastal zones, there is always a strong need for co-operation with local residents and informational and awareness campaigns to inform coastal zone users. Where species or ecosystems in coastal zones are endangered and these measures are not sufficient, the establishment of marine parks can help in the restocking of species, the expansion of knowledge about the dynamics of the ecosystem, the education of the public, and in some countries can potentially be used as a source of income for financing other protection measures through the levying of visitor fees.

Tourism is an important[20] area for further discussion under the Convention on Biological Diversity (CBD), and as coastal zones are the most intensely used ecosystem for leisure, they are particularly influenced by the patterns and pressures of tourism activities. The Conference of the Parties to the CBD are interested in examining the current threats to biological diversity from tourism activities; basic approaches, strategies and instruments that demonstrate where tourism and the conservation and sustainable use of biological diversity are mutually supportive; and the involvement of the private sector, local and indigenous communities in establishing sustainable tourism practices (COP Decision IV/15, point 14, (a)-(c)).

Where tourism activities are responsible for significant pressures on biodiversity in coastal or other biodiversity-rich areas, one of the most promising opportunities for the sustainable use of these resources that has become popular in many countries is the development of markets for eco-tourism or nature conservation. Both of these are important economic sectors which employ biodiversity and nature as inputs. Interestingly, they do not so much employ individual elements of biodiversity as inputs but complete ecosystems. This is particularly true for nature conservation as a special case for a very restricted form of scientific or adventure tourism with relatively high non-monetary costs of access. In general, the tourism industry – particularly nature-based or eco-tourism – has a long-term commercial interest in the conservation and the sustainable use of at least a core of biodiversity resources. As such, tourism offers one of the most promising, robust and important examples of a potentially sustainable use of biodiversity.

Unfortunately, many existing forms of tourism damage biodiversity rather than contribute to its conservation. At least one of the reasons for this is that individual actors disregard the negative externalities that their unsustainable behaviour imposes on the long-term viability of the industry. In order to change unsustainable forms of tourism into sustainable eco-tourism opportunities with high value-added, a number of additional incentives may be necessary. Such incentives can consist of regulations, subsidies, or the creation of licensing systems and the development of strong industry associations.

As with the protection of threatened species, at times it will be necessary or preferable to allocate lands for full conservation rather than trying to manage commercial uses on them sustainably. In this way, both publicly and privately owned parks and nature reserves can provide an important role in conserving ecosystems. Where nature tourism is allowed, charges and entrance fees can be applied in some countries to generate income for the maintenance of the lands.

The development of eco-tourism opportunities does, however, require both a consumer demand for eco-tourism and the co-operation of the tourism developers and operators. For example, while the authorities on the Greek island of Zakynthos tried to encourage this type of market development, the investors on the island did not have access to eco-tourism markets and were already satisfied with the demand and quality of the "traditional" tourism they had access to, so this plan was unsuccessful. However, a recent survey of visitors to the island indicated that a number of tourists noted the poor environmental quality in the area and considered this an impediment to returning for future holidays. Many favoured conservation of the coastal environment and were willing to contribute directly to conservation projects. Thus, the development of local tourist and other business activities which profit from the maintenance of biodiversity values can prove a powerful incentive for gaining the necessary support and co-operation of local industry for the sustainable use of resources.

2. Terrestrial and inland freshwater ecosystems

Biodiversity loss on arable and forested lands, as well as in inland freshwater ecosystems, generally results both from the intensification and expansion of agricultural and forestry practices, and from pressures that arise from industrial and urban development onto these lands. The pressures from land conversion are best tackled through land use planning decisions and enforcement of building regulations. In order to integrate these concerns properly into planning decisions, information about the pressures on biodiversity that arise from the reduction or fragmentation of freshwater ecosystems or arable and forested lands, as well as the expansion of industry and urban growth, needs to be gathered and institutional structures adopted which allow for the consideration of this information by the appropriate decision-makers.

Pressures from agricultural pollution to land, air and water systems can be tackled both through regulatory mechanisms

> **Box V.5. Land-use in OECD countries**
>
> Land-use changes and development possibly exert the most significant pressures on terrestrial ecosystems and on biodiversity in general. With increasing populations and economic growth, many OECD countries continue to experience pressures on biodiversity from urban and industrial growth. Between 1970 and 1995, population levels increased in all but two OECD countries.
>
> This can result in the direct conversion of the lands to other uses, including the fragmentation of previously continuous landscapes by roads and other developments, and can reduce the quality of the lands through the emission of pollutants and interference in natural cycles. Motorway network lengths in OECD countries have, for example, seen a massive increase in recent years, by over 110 per cent between 1970 and 1995.
>
> *Source:*   OECD (1998*b*).

with appropriate enforcement, or through the use of economic incentives to reduce the sources and causes of pollution as well as the emissions themselves.

These pressures result from the neglect of biodiversity, as actors fail to take its value into account, rather than from any deliberate over-use or destruction. This failure results from an inability to extract private value from biodiversity resources through sustainable use of the resources or a lack of awareness of how to do so, such that activities that disregard the multiple values of biodiversity appear more profitable than those that take it into account. Unfortunately, many of the activities that lead to agricultural intensification and expansion – such as the use of fertilisers, pesticides and irrigation water, as well as increased agricultural production in general – are encouraged through government subsidies.

Four distinct strategies offer themselves to policy-makers in these circumstances: first, the dissemination of information about the benefits of biodiversity can facilitate it being taken into account in private decisions; second, regulations and access restrictions can attempt to conserve the most threatened elements of biodiversity at high costs of monitoring and enforcement; third, misguided incentives for land-use and development through tax concessions and infrastructure provision at below cost can be removed; and fourth and perhaps most importantly, alternatives that offer scope for the sustainable utilisation of biodiversity through a mix of market incentives, regulations, compensation for maintaining public existence values and the removal of barriers can be developed.

Arable lands and agriculture

Arable lands provide prime examples of so-called "cultural landscapes", areas which have been shaped by human intervention throughout the centuries. Traditionally biodiversity-rich, arable lands are today mainly used in OECD countries with intensive production methods which have decreased biodiversity. Commercial pressures bearing on agriculture have led to increasing crop specialisation (and thus increased *intra*-species diversity through breeding programmes), but with a concomitant reduction in *inter*-species diversity at the same time, endangering or driving towards extinction particular "land races". Some government regulations contribute to the reduction in agro-biodiversity, including those that restrict lists of the seeds or plants that are approved for trading or human consumption to only a limited range of varieties (Bellegem *et al.*, 1999b). While such restrictions may be necessary for consumer protection purposes, they may unnecessarily restrict organic and other more biodiversity-compatible farming techniques. Care has to be taken that existing biodiversity-rich niches are maintained in combination with uses able to respond to the commercial pressures bearing on agriculture.

Given the large impact of agricultural activities on biodiversity in many OECD countries, and the fact that in some of the densely populated countries of the European Union and in Japan agriculture accounts for more than 50 per cent of the total land area available, the extent and structure of these activities is of great

---

Box V.6.   Facts about arable lands

Characteristics: Arable lands comprise all agricultural lands under permanent crops, crop rotation, meadows or left fallow. They are
often mono-crops and have limited biodiversity.

Size: Arable lands constitute 13.3 per cent of all land area within
OECD countries. These lands have remained fairly stable in
recent years, showing a decrease of only 1 per cent between
1980-95, compared with a world-wide increase of almost
2 per cent.

Economic pressures: Unsustainable agricultural practices, land development/
land use changes, pollution.

Sources: OECD (1997c); World Resources Institute (1996).

---

importance. While agriculture has long been regarded as comparatively more beneficial to biodiversity than other activities – such as industrial production – the
increasing industrialisation and intensification of agricultural activities makes such
distinctions less clear-cut than in the past.

The direct pressures on biodiversity from farming activities are two-fold. First,
there is the increasing tendency to produce a more limited variety of agricultural
crops (species homogenisation). In addition to reducing genetic biodiversity in
general and specifically on the individual farm level, this also reduces the resilience of commercial crops to influxes of diseases, pests and the impacts of climate
vagaries. Second, pressures on biodiversity arise from the direct negative impacts
of intensive agricultural systems on the environment, including the conversion of
biodiverse arable or other lands to more intensive and increasingly specialised
farming systems; the introduction of alien species; effects on soil quality through
pollution from toxic substances such as pesticide and herbicide residues, and
changes in soil biota which maintain soil structure and fertility; increased soil erosion from loss of trees and hedgerows; nutrient and mineral imbalances in water
systems from the leaching of fertilisers; decreased water use efficiency, through the
abstraction of water for irrigation purposes and reduced humidity, precipitation and
recharge of the water table from changes in vegetation and soil structure; the dis-
turbance and fragmentation of the landscape and ecosystems; and effects on air
quality from the release of global (*e.g.* methane from livestock production) and local
(*e.g.* nuisance through malodorous manure application) air pollutants.

However, there are various farming techniques available which are less damaging to biodiversity. For example, organic farming methods can reduce many of the negative effects on the environment, and the micro-ecosystem on organic farms often offers a good refuge for many wildlife species. Other farming practices, such as regular crop rotation, combined agro-forestry systems and multi-cropping, as well as the cultivation of a greater variety of commercial species in general, can also help to maintain biodiversity on arable lands.

Box V.7. OECD agri-environmental indicators

The OECD is developing a set of agri-environmental indicators covering 13 areas – nutrient use, pesticide use, water use, water quality, greenhouse gases, soil quality, land conservation, biodiversity, wildlife habitats, landscape, farm management, farm financial resources, and socio-cultural issues.

The work on indicators, and related quantitative analysis, is aimed at monitoring the state and tracking trends in key environmental areas in the agricultural sector, using and integrating environmental indicators in modelling scenarios of agricultural markets and policies.

Within the well-established Driving Force – State – Response framework, considerable progress has been made on conceptual and measurement issues related to indicators, following a Workshop on agri-environmental indicators held in York, UK in September 1998. A publication (OECD, 1999a) on the results of the workshop is forthcoming.

Agricultural practices like these which allow for richer biodiversity can be encouraged utilising a variety of incentive measures, all of which will be most effective if they address the underlying causes of the specific threats to biodiversity. Thus, there are often fundamental economic failures with respect to the provision of irrigation water, with the existence of direct and indirect (through infrastructure provision) adverse subsidies, and property rights and market failures where rights to water abstraction are not clearly allocated or water prices do not reflect the full social costs of its usage. Often, these economic failures can be corrected. For example, the high levels of government support that agriculture enjoys in many OECD Member countries is being increasingly tied to environmental improvements. Such linkages offer possibilities for the immediate alleviation of pressures on biodiversity and for positive contributions to its conservation and sustainable use through an economically and ecologically sustainable agriculture.

Measures which can be used to provide incentives to address the underlying causes of biodiversity loss from agricultural practices include: the provision of information and training about the appropriate alternative practices, particularly as the farm itself often bears some of the costs of the environmental damage conventional practices result in (and so could benefit from using alternative methods); the taxation of inputs which are environmentally-damaging when used excessively, such as fertilisers and pesticides, to internalise their external damage costs; the removal of adverse subsidies for agricultural intensification; the subsidisation where necessary of environmentally-beneficial activities, such as organic farming or land set-aside; and the creation and promotion of appropriate certification schemes for biodiversity-friendly produce (eco-labelling). Certain forms of agriculture are also considered to have social value *per se*, as well as potentially contributing to biodiversity conservation, including some traditional agriculture and the creation of mosaics of biodiversity habitats. It may be desirable in some cases to offer financial or other support to encourage these practices. Covenants or easements can also be attached to particular land parcels, legally-binding the land owners to undertake or refrain from certain activities. In addition, many OECD countries do not fully enforce the polluter pays principle for agricultural production, and doing so could provide incentives for adopting more sustainable farming practices.

In terms of biodiversity loss, perhaps the largest enforcement problem is that it cannot be easily measured, so increasing the knowledge-base about the interaction between agricultural systems and biodiversity should be a priority (see Box V.7). In addition, because agriculture in many OECD countries is a very traditional and often politically influential sector, it is important to both provide the relevant information to, and consult with, the agricultural stakeholders in order to gain the co-operation necessary for successful implementation of the policies.

Inland freshwater ecosystems

Inland freshwater ecosystems are highly biodiversity-rich and contain a large number of plants, fish, reptiles and insects. As relatively fragile ecosystems, they are under heavy pressure particularly from agricultural activities and the conversion of agricultural lands to other activities. However, these ecosystems have gained new attention through the prominence of water quantity and quality issues on the global agenda, and are now frequently subject to intense and successful policy efforts. They also play an important role in food security (as a major source of protein-rich fish) and in the sequestration of carbon. Inland freshwater ecosystems are now a designated thematic area in the programme of work outlined by the Fourth Conference of the Parties of the Convention on Biological Diversity.

The main direct pressures on biodiversity in these systems arise from the pollution of the water systems by agricultural, industrial and urban wastes and the

---

Box V.8. Facts about inland freshwater ecosystems

Characteristics: Highly biodiversity-rich ecosystems, and relatively fragile. Of major environmental and economic importance, the distribution of freshwater resources varies widely among and within countries.

Size: There are 29 wetlands of international importance in OECD countries that are listed on the Montreux Record of the Ramsar Convention. There is an estimated 8 900 m^3 of annually available internal freshwater resources in OECD countries, representing almost one-quarter of the world total.

Economic pressures: An estimated 11 per cent of total renewable freshwater in OECD countries is currently abstracted for human purposes. Total abstractions increased between 1985-90 by 0.5 per cent. The main quantity pressures on freshwater systems result from abstractions for industrial, agricultural and human consumption, the main quality impacts result from chemical and thermal pollution, disruption of the natural hydrological cycle, agricultural run-off and sedimentation. Competition from invasive species is also a serious problem in some areas.

Sources: OECD (1997c).

---

drainage of water either from the surface for increasing the area available for agricultural production or from groundwater reserves for human, industrial and irrigation purposes. The underlying pressures are the patterns of production and various economic failures, such as the failure of markets to internalise the negative externalities of pollution on downstream water systems. In particular, there is a significant integration failure, whereby the effects of various sectoral activities on inland water systems are not properly considered in the sectoral policy decisions. A particular difficulty arises because of the need to apply measures which conserve not only the immediately identifiable aspects of the resource, but which instead extend to the geographic boundaries of the full water catchment area. Thus, a major problem is the pollution or drainage of these systems by activities that take place either upstream or underground, for example the construction of dams, barrages or water abstraction systems.

For example, the study on the Biebrza River in Poland found that existing conservation measures were inadequate because river catchment boundaries extended beyond the National Park boundaries. Activities undertaken in the areas outside the Park zone were leading to the drainage and the pollution of the river. Similarly, the excessive abstraction of groundwater resources can lead to a lowering of the water table, as was found in the Netherlands case study, and appropriate measures need to be implemented to prevent this. Thus, clearly-defined property rights need to be assigned over all the water resources linked to inland freshwater systems, including those upstream and underground, and measures should preferably be applied which coincide with the geographical boundaries of the resource, not just those aspects which are visible or easily identifiable.

A number of the case studies also emphasised the effects of expanding agricultural and forestry production areas onto wetland ecosystems and the resulting loss of biodiversity. Where this has occurred, it has often resulted in not only a change in the species found in the area, but often also a reduction in species diversity as most agricultural production relies on mono-cropping practices. As discussed in the section on "Reform or removal of adverse incentives" below, the US and other OECD countries employed for many years a range of subsidies to encourage the conversion of wetlands and other biodiversity-rich ecosystems to agricultural or forestry production.

Many of the adverse incentives which encouraged wetlands drainage or the inappropriate use of inland freshwater systems have now been removed, and in many cases other incentives have been implemented to either increase the biodiversity levels on the farm lands or to convert them back to their original ecosystems. Where the adverse subsidies do still exist, however, they should be carefully examined for possible reform or removal.

3. Forests and mountainous regions

Forests

Old-growth forests are, together with inland freshwater systems, one of the most biodiversity-rich ecosystems on earth. A very great number of plants, mammals, birds, reptiles and insects act together to form highly complex ecosystems. In addition to their existence value, forests provide a vital function in the global oxygen-carbon dioxide cycle. Forests provide timber and non-timber raw materials, as well as multiple environmental and social benefits, including protection against soil erosion and natural hazards, ground-water protection, recreation services and scenic values amongst others. The sustainable use of forests has to aim at maintaining the full potential of forests to fulfil their multiple economic, environmental and social functions.

55

Forests are threatened mainly by unsustainable timber extraction, conversion to agricultural land and other land-use pressures, as well as harmful air pollutants such as sulphur-dioxide. Intensive forestry practices can significantly reduce forest biodiversity through the limiting of stands to a single species of often the same age, and the destruction of habitat for other forest-dwelling species through this homogenisation process. Thus, the underlying factors leading to biodiversity loss in forested areas are primarily the patterns of consumption and production, and population growth and distribution.

Box V.9.   Facts about forests

Characteristics: One of the most diverse and widespread ecosystems, forests serve a number of functions environmentally, economically and socially. Complex, renewable, living resource.

Size: Wooded areas constitute 33.5 per cent of all land area within OECD countries. These lands have remained fairly stable in recent years, showing an increase of just under 0.5 per cent between 1970-95, while world wide forest cover reduced by 1.6 per cent. A general trend from mixed, natural forests to mono-cropping ones for production purposes is reducing the quality of forest biodiversity.

Economic pressures: Unsustainable forestry practices, agricultural expansion, conversion to other land uses, and air pollution.

Sources: OECD (1997c).

The increasing frequency of intensely practised wood-production in many OECD countries has led to a loss in forest biodiversity, especially as old-growth forests are substantially reduced. As with the intensification of agricultural production, specific incentives need to be implemented to counter the prevailing economic incentives (sometimes generated by adverse subsidies) to intensify forest production. In Finland, this has been addressed through the use of direct government funds to subsidise sustainable forestry activities on private lands, and the development of a forest certification system.

Both this Finnish case study and the Turkish one highlighted the central importance of gaining the co-operation of the forest users and disseminating the knowledge and skills for maintaining biodiversity by utilising forest products sustainably.

Where forested areas comprise common lands, as in the Turkish study, it is particularly important to allocate property rights over the resources – or at least provide some assurance of long-term continued access for the forest users – in order to ensure appropriate incentives are created for sustainably maintaining the resources over time. Although other incentives, particularly regulatory ones, had been tried before in the Turkish case, it was found that an active programme of practical training and participatory implementation by the forest communities was the most effective method for stopping the illegal felling, grazing and afforestation.

The increase in regulations and restrictions on forestry management practices in recent years, as well as improved understanding of the benefits of multi-use forests, has contributed to forestry practices that are more sustainable. Timber and other forest products are renewable resources which, if managed correctly, can be sustainably harvested and still allow for the existence of significant biodiversity in the forest area. Incentive measures for sustainable forest management have a long tradition, in particular in European countries. Multiple-use forestry offers many opportunities for the integration of biodiversity aspects into the sustainable management of forest resources. However, since concerns for biological diversity are relatively new compared to their "classic" protective and social functions, the development of forestry practices which take into account biodiversity will need further attention.

Efforts to implement appropriate incentives are facilitated where stable property rights are clearly defined over the resources. Certification and eco-labelling schemes have been developed in various countries, and at the international level, which inform buyers of the environmental impacts of the timber they purchase and create markets for sustainably harvested timber. Various economic instruments are used for forestry management in OECD Member countries. Some examples include charges in Austria, Canada, and the Czech Republic related to timber harvests or for not replanting trees, a charge in South Korea for diverting forested areas to other purposes, non-compliance fees in Canada for ensuring forests are harvested and managed sustainably, and subsidies in a range of countries to promote sustainable forestry practices (OECD, 1999*b* forthcoming).

It may also be desirable in some situations to fully conserve forested areas, rather than regulating their sustainable use, especially those that are representative of a particularly rich ecosystem or where it may be expensive or difficult to ensure sustainable forestry practices are used. Thus, while nature-based forestry which attempts to mimic the natural forest structures, processes and dynamics is widely accepted in Denmark as a promising approach to the sustainable management of forest resources, the lack of an adequate scientific basis to support such programmes and the pressure from commercial interests driving forest management have made it difficult to implement such techniques. In order to address the

57

Box V.10.   Forests and climate change

Vegetation withdraws the greenhouse gas CO_2 from the atmosphere through the process of photosynthesis, and returns it through the respiration of vegetation and the decay of organic matter in soils and litter. The most rapid manner to return CO_2 from vegetation to the atmosphere is, of course, burning. Through these processes, land-use changes and forestry practices can have a significant impact on global warming. Processes with net emissions of greenhouse gases are referred to as "sources", processes which result in net removals as "sinks". Sources include the reduction of forests through changes in land-use away from biomass-rich forests or the burning of forest areas. Sinks include the expansion or growth of forest areas.

The net emission or absorption of greenhouse gases due to land-use change and forestry are measured as yearly changes in *stocks* of the gases. The magnitudes involved are considerable: roughly a seventh of the total atmospheric CO_2 passes into vegetation and is returned by respiration each year. For instance, excluding Australia's emissions from land-use and forestry in its 1990 estimates of CO_2 emissions would result in a 45 per cent decrease. Conversely, New Zealand's 1990 emission levels would increase by 81 per cent if the effects of their carbon "sinks" were excluded from the baseline calculations.

Sources: OECD (1998c).

---

wide-spread deforestation that was taking place there, and because relatively few forest reserves existed in the country before 1994, incentives are now being offered for the establishment of strict (untouched) forest reserves on previously privately-cultivated lands.

Again, the key factors identified as essential for the success of this scheme were that it is wholly voluntary, and therefore has the full co-operation of the land-owners, and that these landowners are compensated for the financial losses they incur as a result of no longer utilising the timber resources on the lands set aside as reserves.

Forests are also one of the ecosystems in which direct use values, through timber extraction, hunting and species trade, play a particularly significant role. Hunting and species trade, like fishing, use particular elements of ecosystems for commercial purposes. As such, assigning well-defined property rights over the harvesting or trade of the species, particularly in combination with upper limits on total allowable harvests, can be an efficient incentive measure for ensuring sustainable use of the target species as well as maximising profits from the commercial activities.

Mountainous regions

Mountainous regions, rangelands and semiarid areas are often comparatively biodiversity-poor regions, although some mountain habitats may be rich in biodiversity. The resources are adapted to the very specific environmental conditions of the ecosystems, and as such are generally vulnerable to even small changes in these conditions. They often enjoy high existence values due to the uniqueness of the landscapes and the fauna and flora that grow under the particular and sometimes extreme conditions these landscapes provide. The incentive measures employed in these ecosystems to protect their biodiversity has to reflect their special conditions.

Box V.11. Facts about mountainous regions, rangelands and semiarid areas

Characteristics: Often relatively biodiversity-poor ecosystems and can be fragile.

Size: Permanent grasslands make up 25.3 per cent of total land area in OECD countries, and have been declining since 1970.

Economic pressures: Forestry, agriculture, land development, pollution.

Source: OECD (1997c).

The main pressures on these ecosystems stem from land use changes that result from urban or agricultural expansion. These can lead to the destruction, alteration or division of habitats. Because these ecosystems are often relatively barren, native species tend to require large tracts of continuous ecosystem for survival and regeneration. As a result, pressures on the size and continuity of the ecosystem habitat can have significant detrimental effects on the continued existence of native species.

A further pressure on these ecosystems highlighted in two of the case studies (Mexico and Korea) is the direct, and often illegal, hunting of some of the unique species found in these areas. Because mountainous and semi-arid ecosystems are often found in fairly remote areas, they often suffer from associated access and coverage difficulties. As such, the monitoring and enforcement of hunting restrictions or regulations can be particularly difficult. The Korean authorities found an innovative solution to this, hiring ex-poachers – who were those most familiar with the territory and the black bears requiring protection there – to both track practising poachers and monitor the bear populations.

As the Mexican case study on the conservation of the wild, big-horned sheep (Ovis *canadensis*) indicated, where there are international markets for the hunting of a species, the implementation of a tradable permit system with an initial allocation to local communities can both limit the harvesting of the species and raise local community incomes. By providing private incentives for the conservation of the species by those most likely to harvest it, such an assignment of property rights can also limit the costs of public monitoring and enforcement.

VI. How to Implement Incentive Measures

Since policies aiming at the conservation and the sustainable use of biodiversity have to take into account the multiple causes of biodiversity loss as well as the dual objective of assuring both private and public benefits, careful implementation of the incentive measures plays a key role. Bearing this in mind, this Chapter first discusses three special issues that have to be taken into account in the successful implementation of incentive measures to counter biodiversity loss, and then describes the four phases of implementation with suggestions of how the implementation process can be structured.

1. Three special issues

The multi-dimensionality of biodiversity requires a more extensive process of taking all relevant factors into account in the design of the incentive measures, and a potentially more complicated implementation process due to the multitude of stakeholders. Three elements, in particular, are crucial for the successful implementation of incentive measures for the conservation and the sustainable use of biodiversity:

– information provision,
– capacity building, and
– the involvement of local populations.

While these are all discussed to some extent in Chapter VII as incentive measures in their own right, they are also necessary for the successful implementation of the other incentive measures discussed there. In the design and planning of any measures to promote the conservation or sustainable use of biodiversity resources, complementary policies which fulfil these essential support activities should also be considered.

Information provision

A lack of adequate information is one of the main barriers to the implementation of appropriate incentive measures. In recent years, great efforts have been undertaken, largely under the impetus of the Convention on Biological Diversity, to learn not only about the components of biodiversity, their interactions and the pressures they are exposed to, but also about the possible incentives that are available for positive action for their conservation. Although the elements of biodiversity, the pressures, and the benefits vary in each and every case, links do exist between even the most disparate ecosystems (*e.g.* through migrating birds, atmospheric changes or the transfer of species).

The collection of basic information about the biodiversity resources under threat, the pressures to which they are exposed and the benefits they deliver is a necessary and vital first step to designing appropriate policies for its conservation or sustainable use. The costs in terms of time and resources of gathering this information should not be underestimated, but will often be repaid in the course of the implementation and the management of the incentive measure. The planning process will be improved if clear objectives and priorities have been defined in advance, taking account of the interests of stakeholders. Such information can contribute to the design of the most appropriate measures and the best strategies for implementing them, thus reducing the costs of application, enforcement and monitoring of the measures, and the potential risk of applying insufficient conservation measures.

A particular sub-set of essential information is that which refers to the nature of the incentive measure itself and its effects. Monitoring the responses to the measure *during* and *after* its implementation is an important part of any successful policy. This is therefore reflected in the circular policy process of identifying the pressures on biodiversity, the resulting ecosystem and economic effects, designing and implementing the optimal incentive measures to counter these, then monitoring the responses to these measures, including the remaining and any new pressures on biodiversity. The cyclical framework for the implementation of incentive measures, as developed by Filion (1996) and shown in Box VI.1, runs parallel to the four phases developed in the second part of this Chapter.

Capacity building

Closely related to the assembly and dissemination of information is the creation of adequate capacity for the design, implementation, monitoring and enforcement of incentive measures. Capacity has to be built and nurtured on several levels. While scientific information of high quality is needed in the overall assessment of biodiversity related issues, it is not necessary in each and every single case. In some cases, scientific knowledge and assessments developed for other, similar situations can be drawn upon (see Box VI.2). Neither is it necessary to have expert advice continuously throughout the whole implementation process. In many

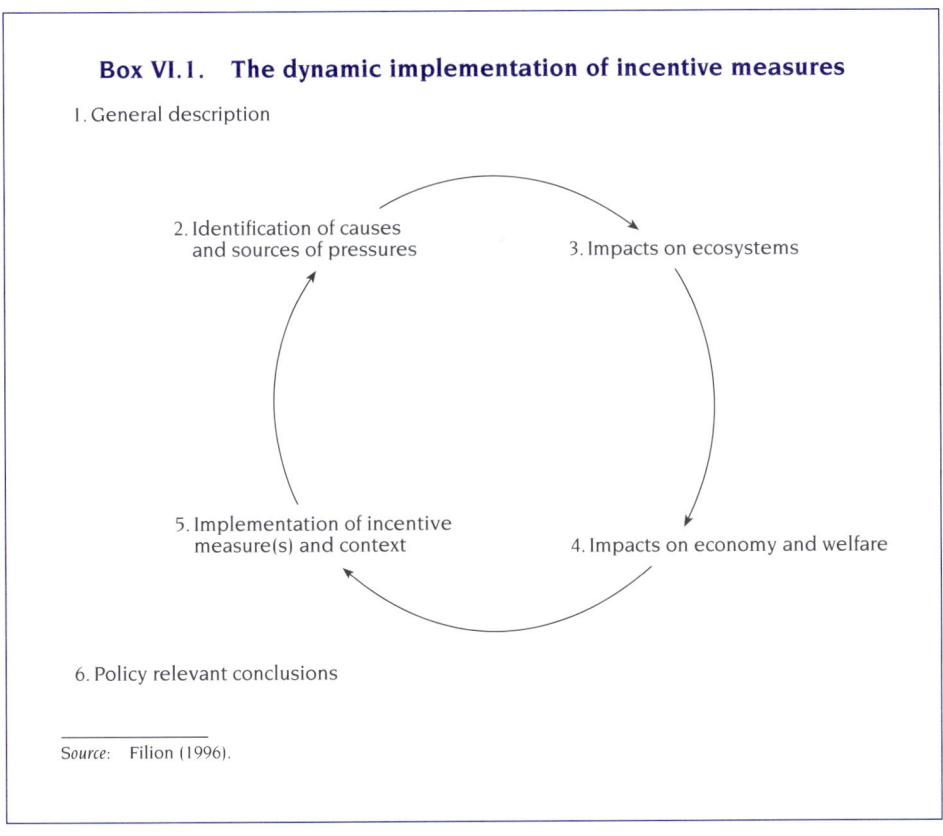

Box VI.1. The dynamic implementation of incentive measures

1. General description

2. Identification of causes and sources of pressures

3. Impacts on ecosystems

5. Implementation of incentive measure(s) and context

4. Impacts on economy and welfare

6. Policy relevant conclusions

Source: Filion (1996).

cases, it is helpful to create appropriate structures to draw on such expert knowledge at critical moments, perhaps with the help of a scientific council, an advisory council or a "group of experts" for the ecosystem in question.

Capacity not only relates to knowledge and conceptual competence. Any kind of incentive measure, whether for biodiversity conservation or otherwise, depends on the existence of an appropriate institutional and legal framework and the corresponding capacity to implement the measure. While the institutional capacity in OECD countries is generally quite strong, attention should be paid to the fact that this does not automatically cover the specific conditions needed for the relatively new policy area of biodiversity conservation and sustainable use. In fact, this is often one of the policy areas where institutional capacity is weakest.

Similarly, while it is not necessary that all actors involved in the implementation of incentive measures are highly qualified experts, some formal training in the basic scientific and economic issues pertaining to biodiversity resources and their

63

Box VI.2.   Environmental Valuation Reference Inventory (EVRI)[21]

The EVRI is a new tool, developed jointly by Environment Canada and the US Environmental Protection Agency, to facilitate the application of *benefits transfer* – the process by which monetary valuations of the benefits of environmental resources (or the costs associated with their loss) can be applied to other, similar situations to reduce duplications in estimating these values.

The EVRI is a internet-based facility which aids analysts in conducting benefits transfers. The user can undertake a customised search of its extensive database of existing non-market valuation studies to find appropriate estimates. New studies can also be entered into the database for future use.

---

conservation and sustainable use is extremely helpful. This type of capacity – the knowledge and skills of the group of individuals who are responsible for designing and implementing the relevant policies – also needs to be strengthened in many countries.

The institutional frameworks in a number of countries are structured such that aspects of the same biodiversity problem are handled at different levels of government or by different departments. This can lead to confusion and the generation of contradictory policies. Whether a particular pressure on biodiversity can be successfully addressed or not will depend to a large extent on which government agencies have responsibility or a legal basis for addressing the different aspects of it, which other bodies are entitled to be consulted, to what extent these agencies and bodies are able to work co-operatively together and whether all aspects of the pressure are actually covered by the assorted jurisdictions of the different agencies.

In order to optimise the efficiency and success with which biodiversity problems are addressed, a coherent and consistent policy approach needs to be developed and fully integrated into biodiversity management at the local, national and, where relevant, international level. Wherever possible, biodiversity goals should also be integrated into other relevant policy areas – such as agricultural or land-use policies – in order to ensure a consistent approach to implementing these goals and to avoid direct policy conflicts (integration failure).

Involvement of indigenous and local communities and stakeholders

The involvement of indigenous and local communities in the management of biodiversity is mandated by Article 8j of the Convention on Biological Diversity which exhorts Parties to *respect, preserve and maintain knowledge, innovations and practices of indigenous and local communities embodying lifestyles relevant for the conservation and sustainable use of biological diversity and promote their wider application with the approval and the involvement of the holders of such knowledge.*

But even without this formal link to the Convention, the participation of local communities can be crucial in determining the success or failure of an incentive measure. There is a public good associated with the kind of biological resource management that some indigenous and local communities practice beyond the direct genetic benefits of maintaining a diversity of species.[22] In such cases, biodiversity policies can be designed to encourage such activities, as well as to learn form them. In addition, it is often the local communities that have the largest stake in the immediate benefits of biodiversity, whether there is an incentive measure in place or not. As they are the stakeholders that may gain the most from the continued existence of the biological diversity, their involvement in the processes that lead to conservation and sustainable use of the biological resources is essential. Because of their strong impact on biodiversity and their direct access to the resources, the involvement of local users can minimise transaction costs and increase efficiency.

While indigenous and local communities are often the main beneficiaries of biodiversity goods, they often also exert significant pressures on biodiversity, and certainly are generally in the best position for implementing and monitoring any necessary measures to relieve these pressures. As such, their involvement in the process, and the full consideration of their interests, are imperative for the success of any incentive measure. Some authors (Young and Gunningham, 1997) have suggested that in order to ensure the success of biodiversity policies, *subsidiarity* – the transfer of authority and the responsibility for implementation to the lowest level at which it can be effectively exercised – is essential. While in some cases the lowest appropriate level may be national, or even international, in many others the most effective level of policy implementation will be at the local level. Often, a mix of local level activities which help to empower and involve local stakeholders and central assistance in the form of the provision of capacity, knowledge and legal and technical support may be most appropriate.

Indigenous and local communities are, of course, not a homogenous group across OECD countries. They range from indigenous people living in more remote areas and with limited direct contact with national policy-making or regulatory systems to communities of residents that are fully integrated into the national social and economic framework. At the same time, there exist other stakeholders who are not necessarily resident locally or even nationally. Ecologists, hunters, researchers, biodiversity prospectors and conservationists are all groups with a special interest in the conservation and the sustainable use of a specific biodiversity resource, and whose interest goes beyond that of the occasional tourist, photo amateur or randonneur, however vital the latter's contributions are to the economic viability of the resource.

Box VI.3. Non-government organisations

NGOs can play an important role in the identification of pressures on biodiversity and the successful implementation of incentive measures for their conservation or sustainable use. They often have extensive informational networks and work in close proximity to the target communities, and as such can respond quickly to identify new pressures in a spontaneous and flexible manner. Because they often operate at a grassroots level, they are receptive of stakeholder views and can be particularly effective in disseminating information rapidly to large sections of the public.

Governments can benefit from the vast array of information NGOs can generate, as well as their representation and involvement of stakeholders and indigenous populations. The success of such co-operation will depend on the degree to which NGOs manage to integrate their activities into the formal government legal and decision-making processes.

As a result, different approaches will be required to involve stakeholders in the implementation process depending on the cultural context. Even within a single area and for a particular problem, more than one type of stakeholder is likely to be found, and they may have conflicting preferences or opinions. For example, while the ecologists, the farmers and the non-farmer residents of the river valley in the French case study all agreed that "something has to be done for the riparian areas of the Garonne", they disagreed strongly on what that "something" was. However, bringing the divergent stakeholders together to discuss the issues is an important first step in the process of identifying the full extent of the problem and what solutions might be available.

The wide range of stakeholders involved in biodiversity conservation is due to the fact that many biodiversity resources have characteristics of a "club good". A club good is a resource that is not private but whose use is exclusive to a certain group of people. While the traditional model assumes the exclusion of outsiders with the help, for instance, of a membership fee, one can think of insiders in the case of biodiversity as people who have invested a particular amount of time and effort into acquiring opportunities to experience the resource. Why is this relevant to the implementation of incentive measures for the conservation and the sustainable use of biodiversity? Because "members" of a club are not only able to "see" the impact of their contribution to the maintenance of the resource (as opposed to public goods) but also because they are frequently highly dedicated individuals who are willing to contribute in exchange for intangible benefits such as "being in the fresh air", or "contributing to conservation".

The involvement of such stakeholder groups in the implementation, monitoring and – under appropriate constraints – enforcement of incentive measures can not only reduce government expenditures, but also provide valuable help in gathering information and assessing benefits. Together with the involvement of local populations, stakeholder involvement is a key element in creating the basis for long-term sustainable use of biodiversity resources.

2. The four phases of implementation

The application of the appropriate incentive measures can be divided into four distinct phases: the identification of the problem, the design of the appropriate instruments, the building of support for the incentive measures, and the introduction, management, monitoring and enforcement of the measures. While in practice some of these phases may be combined, or other aspects may warrant heightened attention, the four phases can structure a first approach by policy-makers to the problem. In general, each case will have to pay attention to these four aspects in one way or another.

Phase 1 – Identification of the problem

In this first phase, policy makers have to decide whether an incentive measure is required or not. It is in this phase that the collection of information about the state of biodiversity, the pressures bearing on it and the benefits that might be forgone by its loss are most important. The involvement of as many groups of stakeholders as possible is desirable, in order to draw on their experiences and expectations and to acquire an understanding of any distributional issues. This can involve experts, local populations, non-governmental organisations, or economic actors whose activities would be affected by any measures taken as well as those currently involved in the biodiversity management.

Often these individuals and groups also play an essential role in bringing the biodiversity threats or pressures to the attention of policy makers in the first place, either through established early-warning procedures or through lobbying and pressure groups. Needless to say, drawing on the experiences of other countries or the results of research in international and inter-governmental organisations such as the OECD is also an important part of this phase of collecting information about the problem and its sources.

67

However, phase one is not only concerned with the *collection* of information about the particular biodiversity resources under discussion, but also with the *dissemination* of this information. In one of the case studies (Netherlands II), it was found that a lack of information on some minor points was no real impediment to making policy decisions, but the most important factor (which is often underestimated) was the inadequate dissemination of what information was available to the appropriate parties. The raising of awareness and, as a next step, the building of coalitions and the assignment of responsibilities are crucial steps in preparing for the implementation of incentive measures. On the basis of adequate information, clear objectives and priorities can then be defined.

Utilising the first rough cost estimates and other available information, policy makers thus decide in phase one not only about the desirability of implementing incentive measures, but also about their principal *feasibility*. In conjunction with this, the relevant stakeholders and experts on the problem under examination should be identified and consultation processes established.

Phase 2 – Design of the incentive measure(s)

As has been discussed above, the multi-dimensional nature of biodiversity, its susceptibility to a wide array of interacting pressures and its impacts on private as well as on public benefits require incentive measures that reflect the particularities of each case. Off-the-shelf solutions – one tax, one regulation, one assignment of well-defined property rights – are unlikely to fulfil the objectives of conservation and sustainable use in a long-term manner. In most cases, combinations of instruments or "hybrid instruments" which satisfy the needs for economic as well as ecological sustainability will have to be employed.

Young and Gunningham (OECD 1997) have identified a series of desirable features of incentive measures for biodiversity conservation or sustainable use which translate to

- predictability of impact,
- conformity to the precautionary principle,
- equity,
- political acceptability,
- economic efficiency,
- adaptability, and
- administrative feasibility.

While such lists can be helpful in highlighting some of the aspects that need due consideration, they should not be interpreted as rigorous checklists. Generally, it will be difficult if not impossible to fully achieve all of these features.

One aspect of political acceptability worthy of note is that the cultural context in which any incentive measure is applied will vary across OECD countries, and sometimes within them as well. As such, different measures will elicit different responses depending on these circumstances and some may be popular in one country while entirely unacceptable in another. For example, the case studies indicate that in some countries (such as Japan and the Netherlands) there may be a strong political need to reach consensus on the issues and work through mutual consultation. In other countries, setting out a clear and legally-binding policy may be more effective.

In general, no single instrument will be flexible and rigorous enough to fulfil all the aspects listed above completely. For example, economic instruments are often insufficient on their own to address irreversabilities in biodiversity, such as species extinctions, but while regulations may be more successful in tackling these particular problems, they are often less economically efficient and regulatory failures are common.

Given the severe consequences of policy failure in this context, and the likelihood that any single instrument will be unable to adequately address all the necessary issues, a mixed approach employing a combination of instruments in a strong institutional framework under the best information available and with the considered involvement of stakeholders and experts is advisable.

As opposed to phase one which requires a wide involvement of different stakeholder groups, phase two will mainly involve experts on incentive measures for biodiversity whether from academe, NGOs, international organisations, or national administrations, all brought together under the direction of the public policy making process. In particular, the combined expertise of these groups can be drawn on at this stage to help determine the main requirements for capacity building, infrastructure needs and more precise cost and benefit estimates where possible in order to better enable policy makers to design appropriate incentive measures for addressing biodiversity loss.

Phase 3 – Building support and providing capacity for incentive measures

Phase three has to translate the intentions of the chosen incentive measures into concrete actions on the ground. Clearly an incentive measure has to be introduced into the context of the already existing legal and institutional framework. Property rights have to be assigned, regulations have to be published, laws have to be enacted, adverse subsidies have to be cut, promoting payments have to be instituted, user fees collected and infrastructure to enable sustainable use activities has to be built. While this moves away from the sphere where international

69

comparisons can provide useful input into national policy making, two elements remain important in every case: the provision of adequate capacity and the involvement of local residents and stakeholders.

The provision of adequate capacity relates to both physical capacity (monitoring equipment, fences, sign posts, etc.) and also to human capacity, *i.e.* the training of staff who can implement and monitor the incentive measure. The provision of institutional capacity is, as has been discussed above, not a significant problem in most OECD Member countries but has to be carefully checked in each case. However, frequently existing institutional frameworks may need to be adjusted or new links forged in order to ensure the multi-dimensional and complex aspects of biodiversity problems are adequately provided for. If the appropriate physical, human or institutional capacity is not put in place from the outset, the incentive measures will be unsuccessful or implemented only at great cost.

As discussed in phase one above, the involvement of local residents and stakeholders can contribute towards – and may be essential for – the identification of threats to biodiversity and the design of appropriate incentive measures. It will also contribute to the building of capacity, and is a necessary step to assure the success of incentive measures in its own right. In addition to providing the most direct and effective link to the implementation, monitoring and enforcement of incentive measures, the involvement of stakeholders and local populations is essential for the building of political coalitions which will often determine whether, and to what extent, new biodiversity threats will be successfully addressed. They can bring both the private and the public aspects of potential biodiversity policies into the political sphere for consideration, and can act as a "checks and balances" system for ensuring the distributional impacts of policies are sufficiently addressed.

As such, the effective communication to the involved parties of the pressures on biodiversity and the appropriate measures available to alleviate these threats is essential. Special educational schemes – including through carefully targeted advertising and information programmes, as well as through environmental education, conservation or national park centres – can promote awareness of the issues with the general public. The use of a common logo or an approved certification scheme for labelling products that are produced in an environmentally sustainable manner can also play a strong role in educating the public and gaining consumer support and confidence. Similarly, the design of green investment fund schemes, as have been set up in the Netherlands, can increase awareness of environmental issues among the general public. All of these schemes also offer economic incentives for producers to utilise environmentally-preferred production processes and to conserve biological diversity.

Governments have an important role to play in setting up and/ or monitoring such certification or eco-labelling schemes, as well as in generally collecting and disseminating relevant information about biodiversity pressures to the wider public in the most effective manner. While these roles may be costly to fulfil at times, some of the expenses related to, *e.g.*, certification schemes can be recouped through appropriation of a portion of the resource rents generated by the scheme. Thus, in the case of the Finnish forestry certification scheme, the costs of the external certification body will be split between the timber buyers and the sellers.

In some cases, it may be possible to combine public and private sector initiatives. This can both help to relieve the government of the administrative burden of designing and implementing the incentive measures, and provide a useful avenue for gaining the support and participation of the private sector in biodiversity conservation and sustainable use. Examples of such co-operation include private sector sponsorship of biodiversity strategies or programmes, and joint research initiatives. In all cases, the stability of the commitment of government over time is an important component in building the necessary confidence in the continuing existence of the incentive measure and in making participants realise the advantages of adapting behaviour.

Phase 4 – Managing, monitoring and enforcing the incentive measures

Phase four might well be the most important of the four phases of incentive measure implementation discussed here. There exists a non-negligible danger that a good incentive measure may be implemented after information has been gathered, experts have been consulted, etc., the responsible policy makers shake hands and return self-contentedly to their administrations – and the incentive measure fails to make any impact towards the conservation or the sustainable use of biodiversity. Monitoring and enforcement of the incentive measure are necessary complements to its design and implementation. In some cases, it can be useful to define from the start a standard review process, to monitor the performance and continuing relevance of the incentive measures on a regular basis. For example, a five-yearly review of the park management plans in the New Zealand study was specified to ensure a regular review of progress would be undertaken.

Part of the successful design of an incentives programme is to set aside sufficient funds for monitoring and enforcing these activities. To some extent, there will always be a trade-off between the success of implementing the scheme and the costs of monitoring and enforcing it, which are necessary in order to achieve this success. The benefits and costs of implementing the incentive measure should be balanced to achieve the optimal level of enforcement and monitoring. Unfortunately, in many cases the administrative costs are judged to be prohibitive without adequate consideration of the benefits the measures would bring.

Of course, the need for and the cost of monitoring and enforcement is not independent of the incentive measure itself. These costs will increase if the incentive measure does not allow for sustainable use, if local residents and stakeholders are not involved, or if distributional impacts from the incentive measure remain uncompensated. This is not to say that these costs may not be incurred anyway. The policy maker, however, will have to balance the costs of enforcement in the absence of economic opportunities through sustainable use with the benefits of conservation accorded to the biological resource, carefully including the non-market and public costs and benefits where possible. The attention does not have to be of the same high level at all times, but the nature of biodiversity will make it the exception rather than the rule that things will take care of themselves even in the presence of the most carefully designed incentive measures. The implementation of an incentive measure is an ongoing dynamic process which requires continuous attention.

An essential part of the ongoing monitoring of incentive measures includes following their effectiveness in reducing the targeted biodiversity threat and any other pressures on biodiversity that may arise either because of them or exogenous circumstances. As such, this leads directly back into phase one of the process, forming a continuous cyclical process of identification of the problem, design and implementation of appropriate measures, enforcement and monitoring, assessment of the effects on the original pressure and identification of new problems, etc.

VII. Experiences with Different Incentive Measures

The twenty-two case studies received from OECD Member countries describe a wide variety of incentive measures for the conservation or sustainable use of biodiversity. The incentive measures presented can be roughly categorised in the following eight groups:[23] fees, charges and environmental taxes; market creation and assignment of well-defined property rights; reform or removal of adverse subsidies; regulations and access restrictions; environmental funds and public financing; information provision and capacity building; economic valuation of environmental benefits and costs; and stakeholder involvement and institution building.

Only the first five groups actually comprise "incentive measures" as traditionally understood, *i.e.* the implementation or abolition of an administrative act by an authority, usually the central government, with a legal grounding and the explicit objective to induce a certain behaviour. Nevertheless, this Handbook has retained information provision, stakeholder involvement, economic valuation, and capacity and institution building in its discussion of incentive measures, while other approaches might have chosen to group them under "framework building".

The special nature of biodiversity as a largely unstructured policy area in which different interests, perceptions and evaluations interact, frequently makes the conceptual distinction between incentive measures and their context of implementation unnecessary and even unrealistic at times. Instead, both the measures and their context tend to evolve at the same time, with distinct choices and policies determining the context in which the measures are implemented as much as the choice and application of the measures themselves. For example, markets can only arise where property rights are defined and enforced. An environmental tax can only be sensibly introduced if information about causes and impacts has been established.

The most important advantages and disadvantages of each incentive measure are discussed below, with examples drawn – where possible – from the case studies which examined these incentive measures in different contexts. The aim is not to provide an exhaustive overview of the case studies, but rather to discuss the dif-

OECD 1999

ferent incentive measures in light of the illustrative material provided by the case studies.[24] In particular, the use of different combinations of incentive measures is highlighted in Section 4. Only a few of the case studies actually considered a single incentive measure in isolation. The complexity of biodiversity, the multitude of its stakeholders and its combination of private and public values make the use of a set of complementary incentive measures the norm rather than the exception.

1. Economic incentives – making the market work for biodiversity

The idea of economic incentives is linked to the concept of rational individuals who maximise their private well-being. Governments are called upon to implement incentive measures in those cases in which private utility-maximisation causes imperfect outcomes, as individuals do not take into account the impacts of their activities on the well-being of other individuals or the public at large. This state of affairs is referred to as the 'existence of an externality'. To the extent that people interact with each other in the context of markets, and these markets are unable to include the externality in their pricing signals, the existence of an externality is also referred to as a "market failure".

Externalities or market failures exist when an activity undertaken by one individual or group of individuals has a (positive or negative) affect on another individual or group, and those affected neither compensate (if it is a positive externality) nor are compensated (if it is negative) by those undertaking the activity for the generation of these "external effect". In such cases, those who are affected by the actions of others are unable to factor the external effects into the decision-making of those responsible for the activity. The reasons for this lack of feedback mechanism can be ignorance of the exact causal relations between the activity and the external effects, the difficulties of transmitting this information, the costs of co-ordination and transaction associated with transmitting the information or negotiating a payment for the externality between the parties, or the absence of clearly-defined property rights or the legal infrastructure to enforce these rights. Appropriate government policies can be designed to compensate for the lack of a feedback mechanism and to safe-guard the interests of those that are negatively affected.

Frequently, externalities exist in cases where it is not possible to identify the particular individuals who are negatively affected by the actions of others but where so-called "public goods" which accrue to society at large are affected. This holds particularly in the case of biodiversity. If a given ecosystem disappears, the negative impact on each individual might be too small to warrant individual action, but nevertheless the total impact, due to the large number of individuals affected, might be considerable and require policy intervention.

Environmental economists and regulators have developed a large number of possible solutions for the problem of externalities, including the imposition of artificial shadow prices in the form of environmental taxes or charges which reflect the damage to public goods, the better definition of property rights with the enabling markets, and the subsidisation of behaviour more sympathetic to public interests. One of the most cost-effective means of safe-guarding biodiversity is in fact the abolition of *existing* interventions which support activities which impose negative externalities, such as subsidies to economic sectors which exert pressures on biodiversity.

Most of these instruments have been studied and developed in the context of environmental pollution. The case for government intervention in such circumstances is straightforward: governments have superior information and vastly reduced transaction costs in ensuring that public health and amenity considerations are adequately reflected in the actions of large manufacturing industries. A tax, charge, standard or subsidy can frequently solve the problem (or reduce its impact significantly), while, in the absence of government intervention, the consequence would be either inaction or a myriad of small-scale liability suits with protracted arguments and great difficulty establishing any objective basis for decision-making.

The situation concerning the conservation or the sustainable use of biodiversity is comparable but not identical. This is due to the fact that the costs imposed by the loss of biodiversity are frequently of a different nature than the relatively more straightforward costs connected with pollution. Of course, the loss of biodiversity often imposes costs which can be fully internalised by appropriate government action, such as for the water purification services of a functioning ecosystem.[25] Frequently, however, the value of biodiversity resides in its pure existence, or possibly in its – as yet still unknown – future uses. In these cases, the logic of applying economic instruments to correct for externalities and market failures is put to severe tests. Which parts of biodiversity are most worthwhile preserving? According to which criteria shall trade-offs be made?

Economic instruments designed to correct for market failures do not loose their effectiveness in such circumstances but can at times not account for the *complete* solution of the problem which requires additional information and institution-based interventions. Member countries have presented a wide array of experiences with economic and regulatory incentives which are discussed below. Following this, Sections 2 and 3 discuss those supporting policy interventions which complement economic incentives in light of the particular challenges posed by the loss of biological diversity.

OECD 1999

Fees, charges and environmental taxes

A range of economic instruments are used in OECD countries to encourage environmentally preferred activities. These include charges or non-compliance fees to forestry activities to ensure harvesting activities are undertaken at sustainable levels, liability fees for the rehabilitation or maintenance of ecologically-sensitive lands, the application of fishing license fees or taxes, the application of levies for the abstraction of groundwater, and charges for the use of public lands for grazing in agriculture, for the use of sensitive lands (such as the Great Barrier Reef in Australia), for the hunting or fishing of threatened species, or in natural parks for tourism activities (OECD, 1999*b* forthcoming). However, there frequently exists great confusion pertaining to the distinction between environmental taxes, fees, charges and levies. Box VII.2 below therefore reproduces the standard OECD definitions.

Box VII.1.   Facts about environmental taxes

Description:	Price-based incentive measures which aim to internalise external costs; generate revenues for environment-related objectives or actions; and apply charges for resource use.
Advantages:	Maximise economic efficiency; easily understandable.
Disadvantages:	Rely on measurability of single components and on agreement about external costs values; can require extensive monitoring.
Applicability:	Applicable in situations where impacts are easily measurable (*e.g.* hunting) and sources of impacts can be easily monitored.

In some cases, rather than issuing non-compliance fees or holding companies liable for the rehabilitation or restoration of habitats after exploitation, some countries have opted to ask for performance bonds from the outset. These can be required of private enterprises or individuals before undertaking certain activities to act as a guarantee that they will comply with specified requirements. Examples of performance bonds in use in OECD countries include those levied on mining operations in Australia, Canada and the US committing the owners to the satisfactory rehabilitation or reclamation of the sites, and bonds required of hazardous waste sites in Canada to ensure the safe disposal of the waste in case the operating company becomes insolvent (OECD, 1999*b* forthcoming).

The use of fiscal instruments for biodiversity protection is based on the idea that the social costs of biodiversity loss can be imputed into the price of the activ-

---

Box VII.2.   Environmentally related taxes and charges

Taxes

The OECD classification (Publication Revenue Statistics) defines taxes as "compulsory, unrequited payments to general government. Taxes are unrequited in the sense that benefits provided by government to taxpayers are not normally in proportion to their payments." Note that a tax (unrequited) can be earmarked if it is decided that a certain percentage of the revenue will be affected to a specific purpose (*e.g.* when part of the gasoline tax is earmarked to building roads).

Charges/fees

The OECD classification also uses the terms "fees" and "user charges" (as opposed to "taxes") without giving a precise definition of these terms. In practice, the terms charges and fees are often used interchangeably. Therefore, charges and fees are defined as compulsory requited payments to either general government or to bodies outside general government, such as for instance an environmental fund or a water management board. Thus in return for a charge or a fee, a service is provided in proportion to its magnitude.

Levies

The general term "levy" covers *all* types of compulsory payments. Note that, according to the OECD classification there are "borderline-cases" where a levy could be considered as "unrequited", *i.e.* as a "tax" (if the payment is made to "general government" as opposed to a charge or fee). Examples exist when the levy exceeds the cost of providing the service or when the payer of the levy is not the receiver of the benefit (at least not in proportion to his contribution, such as, *e.g.* a levy paid by timber companies to promote the consumption of sustainably harvested wood (Personal communication, Nils Axel Braathen, OECD Environment Directorate, 1998)).

---

ities that cause this loss. Conversely, this implies that activities that are socially beneficial should enjoy lower overall taxes. In both cases, this requires the monetary measurement of the preferences for the public good aspects of biodiversity. Once the correct values have been derived, economic instruments can achieve economic and ecological efficiency.[26] However, while the determination of exact monetary values for biodiversity is feasible in principle on the basis of techniques developed by economic theory, the intrinsic complexity of biodiversity makes this very difficult to accomplish in practice.[27]

A number of studies, including three of the present case studies (from Canada, Korea and France – described in detail in the section on "Economic valuation as incentive measure and support for decision-making" below, have taken up the challenge of determining the social costs of biodiversity loss or the benefits of its conservation in monetary terms, illustrating that valuation is possible and defensible. However, the large degree of uncertainty and incompleteness associated with such estimates makes it very difficult to use them for such an exact exercise. As a result, fees, charges and environmental taxes are rarely used to exactly internalise the full social costs of activities.

For example, an exercise was undertaken in the Garonne Valley in France to determine how much farmers would be willing to accept in compensation for conserving land around the river and how much residents would be willing to pay them to do so. While it was found that the conservation was worth a significant amount to local residents (their willingness to pay for it would cover 25 years worth of compensation to the farmers), the study emphasised that such estimates were seldom used to develop appropriate economic instruments. It was found that biodiversity protection was seen instead as "a more general reference than a precisely defined objective" (Amigues and Desaigues, 1998; 11).

Because of these difficulties, economic instruments – particularly in the biodiversity policy arena – are often designed for other purposes than to fully internalise external costs. While examples exist of economic instruments designed for this purpose in other areas,[28] the difficulties surrounding the identification and quantification of the externalities associated with biodiversity loss imply that the internalisation of external effects is generally not the purpose of economic instruments applied in this field. A further general problem with the application of economic instruments for environmental purposes exists due to the resistance of finance ministers, who often have the legal responsibility for them, but dislike the uncertainties regarding the revenue base of such instruments.

The purpose of economic instruments is more often to meet certain agreed environmental targets through their incentive effects (as was the case in the French case study cited above), to cover the transactional costs of conservation through their revenues (such as through setting national park entrance fees to pay for park maintenance), or to reduce a pricing differential which is biased against environmentally friendly alternatives (such as by introducing a levy on the development of greenfield sites and perhaps a corresponding subsidy to the rehabilitation and development of brownfield sites, as suggested in the UK study on heathland management).

In another example, the German case study (Popp, 1999) found that visitors fees, nature taxes and conservation or exploitation levies could be useful instruments for not only internalising some of the environmental pressures on two biosphere reserves from human activities, but also for generating enough income to cover the advertising and maintenance of the reserves. Thus, the Rhön biosphere reserve generated DM 40 000 in visitor's fees in 1997, one-quarter of which was spent on advertising. In other areas, a special "nature tax" is deducted from the visitor's tax to directly finance environmental measures. There are also proposals for a conservation or exploitation levy as well.

Many direct and indirect subsidies to environmentally preferred activities can be seen as creating a deliberate pricing differential in favour of these activities, or correcting for an existing price differential which favours less preferred activities. The size of the economic incentive is normally determined by the gap between the profitability of the competing sustainable and unsustainable activities, rather than by any measurement of social *preference* for the benefits which are *a priori* assumed to exceed the costs of achieving them.

Thus, the Dutch government introduced a tax on groundwater abstraction in 1995 to counter the desiccation effects (one of the most important causes of biodiversity loss in the country) that had resulted from the excessive use of groundwater reserves (Bellegem *et al.*, 1999*a*). Most provinces also implement their own small groundwater abstraction levies as well. In addition to internalising some of the costs of the desiccation, these taxes and levies also raise the *relative* costs of water abstracted from ground reserves compared with the less environmentally damaging use of surface water. Without this price differential, the cost of using surface water tends to be more than that associated with groundwater usage, but with the taxes and levies, at some point the price differential turns and it becomes economically favourable to switch to surface water.

Market creation and assignment of well-defined property rights

The creation of markets through the removal of barriers to trading and the assignment of well-defined and stable property rights is based on the premise that rational holders of these property rights will maximise the value of their resources over time. The underlying reasoning is that if biodiversity resources were thus privatised, their conservation would be better assured than under open access regimes where users often resort to short-term exploitation on a first-come, first-serve basis.

This reasoning holds well for biodiversity resources that contain private market value such as commercially valuable fish-stocks, the tradable meat, skins or other attributes of certain animals, or other biodiversity resources such as commercially valuable timber and non-timber forest products. As a result, the assignment of well-defined property rights has been extensively employed in connection with the management of commercial fish stocks in the form of individual transferable quotas, as well as private ownership of forested lands. Perhaps the largest drawback of the assignment of property rights as an incentive measure for the conservation and the sustainable use of biodiversity, whether to individuals or groups, relates to the fact that the incentive for the owners to sustainably manage their resources extends

79

Box VII.3.   Facts about market creation

Description: Markets can be created through the clear definition of property rights over resources or their use, and the allowance of trading in these rights.

Advantages: Result in the most efficient allocation of resources between competing users, and generates appropriate prices for them; low monitoring requirements.

Disadvantages: May be imperfect where there are (large) external effects and/ or monopolies.

Applicability: Where clearly defined property rights can be established and upheld for easily identifiable goods and services, and transaction costs are low enough and interested parties numerous enough to allow regular trade.

---

only to the privately appropriable elements of biodiversity. Existence values of species that are not commercially valuable and the surrounding ecosystem will not be taken into account without further regulations or other incentive measures.

But the maximisation of net present value from private activities can sometimes have positive spillover effects as well, albeit only for those elements of sustainable development whose value is privately appropriable or which are intrinsically linked to such elements. For example, private income from forested areas is often maximised through the long-term maintenance of the forest for ongoing timber extraction, which also leads to the positive externality of realising the forest's existence value.

Because private forest owners have a financial interest in maintaining a stock of trees for continued timber harvesting, the allocation of private property rights over biodiversity-rich resources is common in forested areas. As such, two of the case studies examined the allocation of private property rights over forested areas, emphasising the benefits that can be gained from local communities holding the property rights to the resources requiring conservation or sustainable use. The Turkish case study (Arançli and Stevens, 1999) discussed how encroachment, illegal felling and grazing, and afforestation have led to degradation of forest ecosystems and infertile, eroded soils. Recognising these problems, the local authorities have implemented a participatory project on community forestry, attempting to simultaneously improve the quality of life in the community and the forest ecosystem. It was noted that while the forest remained a common resource, it was open to over-exploitation by villagers who had little incentive to practice sustainable harvesting techniques so long as they were uncertain whether they would be able to utilise the resulting resources at a later date, and thus capture some of the benefits of sustainable behaviour. The assignment of rights that allow the villagers to continue using the forest resources provide the necessary incentives for them to seek to sustainably manage them.

The allocation of well-defined property rights can also be an effective means for increasing local community incomes while conserving or sustainably using the particular endangered species. They allow for the realisation of the full, privately-appropriable use values of the biodiversity resources. In Korea, it was found that the most effective means for preserving the Mount Chiri National Park and the Asiatic black bears that reside there was to ensure that they become profitable to the local community, thus providing an incentive for their sustainable use and conservation by the people in the strongest position to do so.

In Mexico, a well-designed and highly innovative approach to the sustainable management of the big-horned sheep (*Ovis canadensis*) has been implemented, in the form of tradable permits for the rights to hunt the sheep. The government sets a sustainable hunting level, and allocates tradable permits to the local communities up to this quota. Given the high international demand for hunting the species, it is expected that permits can easily double or triple their value on the international market, and thus provide an important source of income for the local populations. As such, this scheme provides both effective incentives for the sustainable use of the sheep, and has the co-operation of the local people. While there have been some difficulties with the implementation of the scheme, the Mexican government are now working to overcome these. The example shows once more how closely linked are the implementation of the incentive measure *per se* and the creation of the appropriate information and capacity.

Such tradable permits have the dual benefits of being able to both guarantee environmental effectiveness (*e.g.* through specifying the allowable number of kills under a hunting permit scheme) and encouraging the most economically efficient methods of undertaking the permitted activity (as compared with regulations which restrict certain activities or methods of undertaking these activities through, for example, specifying allowable fishing or hunting methods). Theoretically, the permits will be traded until they are allocated to those who will realise their highest value.

However, in order to implement a tradable permits scheme or to create another type of market for biodiversity goods and services, there must be a clear assignment of property rights. In fact, the lack of properly defined property rights is often identified as one of the main underlying causes of biodiversity loss. This was clearly one of the main reasons for poor management of the biodiversity resources

Box VII.4.   Individual Transferable Quotas (ITQs) for fisheries management

Fisheries are often open-access resources where the social costs of overfishing are not internalised in the fishing activity. In an open market, fishing effort will tend to increase past the point of maximising fishing income to the point where all positive profits to be garnered as rent from the resource are dissipated. As this may not occur until a harvest level above the maximum sustainable yield, this can lead to over-fishing of the target species and even the collapse of the commercial industry. Therefore, incentive measures to restrict fishing activities are often necessary.

The essential cause of this pressure is the non-existence of property rights over fisheries resources, but assigning property rights over marine areas is generally not feasible (except with stationary species such as shellfish beds). However, property rights can be assigned over the harvesting of the commercial species themselves through ITQs. These guarantee the holder the right to harvest a certain percentage of the total allowable catch for the season, and are the most direct mechanism for addressing these problems. In addition to the environmental benefits of limiting catch to a sustainable level, ITQs are often used to increase the economic efficiency and profitability of the fisheries (in theory they should lead to the maximisation of total income from the fishery) as well, or to stabilise fishing employment.

A case study on ITQs produced for this *Handbook* found that while allocating individual, tradable property rights for the use of fishery stocks can be an effective measure for managing the target species, ITQs by themselves might not be sufficient to protect other species or the surrounding ecosystem. Where ITQs are used to allocate fishing rights to a particular species, complementary measures are often necessary to conserve and sustainably use the surrounding ecosystem. A particular problem which has to be addressed is high-grading, the practice of discarding the smaller, often young fish and keeping only the high-grade ones to count against the quota. This can be addressed by measures such as observers, mandatory landings, improved gear selectivity and prohibitions. There are also social concerns to be addressed, particularly equity issues relating to the initial allocation of ITQ rights, and the possibility that the use of ITQs may lead to the elimination of small-scale fishers or reduced employment and crew income.

Thus, while ITQs can be a valuable incentive for increasing fishery profits while harvesting sustainable levels of a particular fish species, they are most effective when accompanied by other enforcement and regulatory measures – such as limits of days at sea, number and size of gear units, and conditions on gear and vessels – to ensure their social and environmental compatibility.

Source: Gudmundsson *et al.* (1998).

in the Garonne Valley in France (Amigues and Desaigues, 1998). While the State is responsible there in principle for the management of the river itself and the "regularly flooded areas" around it, it is generally difficult to clearly delineate which areas are regularly flooded and the river regularly changes course, so these areas vary naturally.

As a result, the authorities have often been ineffective in enforcing these rights and the riverbanks, along with the ecological services they provide, have been under severe pressure from the riparian landowners. To counter these difficulties, the authors of the case study recommended a redefinition of the property rights around the river and examined the possibility of a "transfer" of some of the riparian lands to the public through the payment of compensation by the public to the landowners for ceasing agricultural and other activities along the riverbanks.

An unusual problem of residents claiming property rights over biodiversity-rich lands was reported in the Greek study, where all cadestral and ownership records for the island of Zakynthos were destroyed in an earthquake in 1953. Since then, residents have submitted ownership claims to sand dunes, wetlands and the forests which usually comprise public or community owned land, and the courts have upheld some of these claims. A number of ownership claims have not been brought to the courts as yet and their pending state may be an obstacle to applying a new tool for acquisition of land by the State within protected areas.

In some cases, where incentives have not been applied or were found to be insufficient for the sustainable use or conservation of biodiversity resources on private property, programmes for a transfer of property or use rights to the public have been utilised. Some examples include the purchase of biodiversity-rich areas for conversion to protected parks or reserves, as has been carried out by many governments or environmental non-government organisations, or programmes for the purchase of wetlands for protection and agricultural lands for the restoration of wetlands.

However, public ownership of lands is not a guarantee for sustainable management. One of the case studies (Naskali, 1999) found that the majority of extensive clear cutting of Finnish forests has taken place on state-owned lands, while the smaller, family-run holdings often use integrated forest management techniques which sustainably utilise other non-timber aspects of the forest ecosystem as well, such as for berry picking, fishing, hunting and recreational uses. In Denmark, a law used to be in place which prohibited the unproductive use of major forest areas on private or public land, and thus impeded the establishment of biodiversity rich old-growth forests (this law was reformed in 1989). In fact, it was found that private forests in Denmark were often those with the most biodiverse ecologies. However, public ownership of natural resources facilitates the integration of public objectives through the political process, whereas private ownership, other things being equal, tends to concentrate on the efficient exploitation of direct use values.

Box VII.5. Tradable (transferable) development rights

While property law in some countries is based on the indivisibility and absolute nature of land ownership (such as in Western Europe or Japan), in others (such as in North America) land ownership is a "bundle" of different use rights, some components of which can be treated separately. Where this is the case, some aspects of use rights can be traded between interested parties, while the remainder are held by the original owner(s).

For example, NGOs, individual conservationists or the government may acquire certain aspects of a land parcel, such as development rights, in order to conserve biodiversity, while all other use rights remain with the land owner.

Vice versa, regulatory constraints on land development can strongly affect the price of land, and in some cases compensation for such restrictions is offered in the form of development rights on other plots of land. For example, a number of states in the US allow the trading of "easements", development rights which are detachable from a given piece of land and usable on another property. These are often employed with express environmental objectives, limiting the type and amount of development activities in a particular zone, but allowing "trading" of these rights to allocate where the development takes place.

In Greece, for example, to compensate for the strict building development restrictions placed on properties in a Nature Reserve created in 1990 on the island of Zakynthos, other parts of the coast were designated as tourism development areas under a Land Use Master Plan.

Sources: Renard (1998); Spyropoulou and Dimopoulos (1999).

Once the conservation of the ecosystem has been achieved through public ownership and management, certain sustainable use rights can in some cases then be leased or sold to private developers. Similarly, a number of the case studies highlight the use of *partial* transfers of use rights to restrict activities on ecologically sensitive private lands, rather than transferring full ownership to government bodies or NGOs. These can include restrictions on development (*e.g.* such as through the use of permits), or by implementing legally-binding property covenants or land management plans which restrict activities on private lands to the sustainable use of the biodiverse resources.

Such measures can be seen as transferring some of the development or use rights associated with the privately-owned land to the government or to an environmental body. They depend on the institutional and informational capability of governments to define and communicate the different components of property and use rights, which can then be traded in the form of covenants or development rights. For example, a permitting system has been introduced in the Netherlands for the abstraction of groundwater, transferring the property rights for the use of groundwater from the public commons to the government, which then has the authority to permit abstraction where sustainable and for purposes that are deemed appropriate (Bellegem *et al.*, 1999*a*).

Permits can also be allocated for the right to emit certain pollutants, limiting the total quantity of pollution and allowing trade between polluters to ensure the most efficient allocation of these rights. Such schemes exist for air pollution in the US and Canada, for saline emissions to the Hunter Valley river in Australia, and for effluent discharge to the Lower Fox River in the US (OECD, 1999*b* forthcoming).

In another example, property owners in Victoria, Australia need a permit to clear native vegetation over a certain size limit. In addition, the Revolving Fund for biodiversity established by Trust for Nature Victoria in Australia is used to purchase land with special conservation significance, upon which a covenant is then placed to ensure the future sustainable use of the land, before it is resold to sympathetic individuals (Carter, 1999). In this way, the Fund is able to transfer biodiversity-rich properties to those individuals whose use will be most likely to be compatible with the conservation of the resources. In some senses, the Fund "purchases" the right to prohibit or restrict certain damaging activities on the property as proscribed in the covenant agreement. Similarly, the Danish study found that a programme in Denmark to transfer privately cultivated forest areas into strict forest reserves has emphasised the use of "permanent management agreements", based on grants provided for forestry offsets as well as voluntary co-operation by private owners.

Because these activities are voluntary and compensated, the measures gain the support of those who are ultimately responsible for ensuring the protection or sustainable use of the lands: their private owners. In addition, the implementation of such measures can be less costly for the government (and hence taxpayers) than the full transfer of the land to a publicly managed reserve or park, or attempting to enforce and monitor regulations or access restrictions with which the private land owners are not sympathetic. The more pervasive and the more clearly defined such use rights are, the more easily they lend themselves to trading in newly established markets in which governments and NGOs can safeguard public existence values through their participation in market transactions.

Reform or removal of adverse incentives

The reform or removal of support for activities that exert pressure on biodiversity is one of the most promising incentive measures for the conservation and the sustainable use of biodiversity. The removal of such "adverse incentives" not only alleviates pressures on biodiversity, but can also increase economic efficiency and reduce government budget deficits (see OECD, 1998d).[29] Subsidisation comes in many forms, from direct payments and market price support to credit guarantees, technical assistance and the provision of free infrastructure allowing easy access to biodiversity-rich areas. A number of the case studies discussed government support policies which directly or indirectly contributed to a loss in biodiversity. While many of these adverse subsidies have been removed, some still remain.

Box VII.6.   Facts about the reform or removal of adverse subsidies

Description:	Subsidies can encourage activities that have negative effects on the environment and biodiversity conservation.
Advantages:	Reforming or removing these incentives can lead to an easing of pressures on the environment, improved economic efficiency and reduced fiscal expenditures.
Disadvantages:	Adverse subsidies can often be difficult to identify (lack of transparency); and may be politically difficult to reform because of strong opposition by the recipients.
Applicability:	Where clear benefits in terms of budgetary, economic efficiency and/ or environmental goals can be identified, and potential compensatory measures exist to facilitate the support removal process.

A large number of the adverse subsidies examined were the result of government support programmes to agriculture, which is probably the most common form of support in OECD Member countries. Some of the most egregious examples of adverse regulations and incentives to agriculture exist in the US where a range of federal and state incentives have encouraged wetland loss, including the provision of direct financial support to landowners for the explicit purpose of draining wetlands up until the late 1970s (see Box VII.7 for further details). Other case studies also identified adverse incentives which discouraged sustainable agricultural practices, including:

- the Austrian case studies (Hubacek and Bauer, 1999; Hoppichler and Groier, 1999) also found government support for wetland drainage for agricultural cultivation and other subsidies which encouraged agricultural production and intensification;

- the Korean study (Shin and Shon, 1999) found support for conversion of forests to agricultural land;

– in Denmark it was illegal until 1989 to leave forest areas unproductive (Danish Ministry of Environment and Energy, 1999);

– Finland used to administer a range of subsidies for the production and export of timber, although many of them were removed under the 1997 Financing of Sustainable Development Act (Naskali, 1999);

– New Zealand had two direct subsidies to farmers to clear their lands of indigenous forest until 1984, as well as minimum price support for agricultural produce which encouraged intensification and over-production (Hutching, 1999);

– Australia provided large tax reductions for land clearance until recently (Carter, 1999);

– a Canadian Task Force in 1994 identified various disincentives in the taxation system with respect to biodiversity conservation (Rubec, 1999); and

– a number of the case studies discussed the adverse effects of government provision of infrastructure without full-cost recovery, such as roads to remote areas for timber harvesting or agricultural development, and irrigation or wetlands drainage equipment.

A particular case is constituted in the European Union by the Common Agricultural Policy which continues to support agricultural producers, by an estimated 43 per cent of the total value of production in 1996 (OECD, 1997e). Five case studies, two on the Netherlands, and one each on Austria, the United Kingdom and France, discussed the negative impacts of these agricultural subsidies on biodiversity. In addition to production-linked market price support policies which encourage the use of intensive agricultural practices and the expansion of agricultural land into heathlands and other biodiversity-rich areas, these studies identified other adverse subsidies to research and development, fuel for agricultural use, machinery and investment support including for irrigation equipment, provision of infrastructure for draining agricultural lands, and low VAT rates for agricultural inputs.

These subsidies are often biased in favour of environmentally-damaging farming practices, for example by encouraging the excess use of agricultural inputs, or by allowing agricultural costs to be income tax deductible, while conservation practices are not. While many of these subsidies are being reduced, this is often a slow political process. Alternatively, a number of subsidies are now being reformed to link them to the undertaking of specific activities with positive environmental impacts, such as land set-asides (under certain conditions), reductions in the use of pesticides or fertilisers, the maintenance of hedges and field borders as semi-natural habitats and the increased use of organic farming techniques (see the section "Environmental funds and public financing" for further details).

87

Box VII.7. Wetlands in the United States – a history of adverse incentives

In the mid-1800s, US Congress gave almost 65 million acres of wetlands to 15 States under the Swampland Acts to enable these States to reclaim their wetlands through the construction of levees and drains to reduce flooding. Nearly all of these lands were then transferred to private ownership, and many have since been converted to other uses. Since then, a range of other Federal programmes have provided incentives for wetland loss, including reservoir construction for flood control, irrigation and hydroelectric power, road development projects, flood disaster relief and insurance, subsidies and tax incentives for forestry and agriculture, and grazing policies on federal lands. Some of these policies include:

- Federal assistance for the draining of wetlands for production of subsidised crops and the expansion of arable land;
- the US Department of Agriculture shared the costs of wetland drainage with farmers up until the late 1970s, and the US Army Corps of Engineers has been rechannelling rivers for flood control and agricultural drainage since the 1870s;
- prior to 1985, US farm price and income support programmes also encouraged wetland conversion, as price support encourages the use of marginal lands; and
- prior to 1986, wetland conversion investments were also favoured in the Internal Revenue Code in a number of specific ways, as expenses for land clearing, drainage, and land shaping could be deducted from farm income and tax deductions were available for machinery used in wetland conversion under accelerated cost recovery schemes.

While most of these direct and indirect subsidises to wetland conversion have now been removed, they contributed to the conversion of nearly half of the US wetlands to other uses since 1780. To counter these effects, the government is now employing positive incentives ("environmental stewardship payments") for the conservation of existing wetlands and the conversion of some agricultural lands back to wetlands.

Source: Heimlich, et al. (1999).

In Laganas Bay, Zakynthos, Greece, where the potential for high levels of tourist activity was identified as a threat to the nesting grounds of the loggerhead turtle, the case study indicated that nation-wide government incentives for the almost unconditional development of small "rooms to let" hotels has had a negative impact in the area, even though they were applied under the specific provisions of the local land use plans.

As discussed in the study on ITQs and the sustainable management of fisheries, many countries also significantly subsidise their fishing fleets through market price support, subsidies to fishing gear and boats, barriers to trade, provision of infrastructure and government services. Some of these subsidies may reduce the costs of harvesting the fish. Their impacts on marine resources are currently being examined in various different international fora, including the WTO, FAO, APEC, and the OECD Fisheries Committee.

While all government support is linked to underlying political or social rationales, many existing subsidy programmes were developed at times when concerns for biodiversity were markedly less developed than today. Their review and potential removal thus constitutes a real possibility and is already underway in some countries and sectors. Many OECD countries have been reforming their fisheries and agricultural subsidies to make them less environmentally-damaging, even linking some of them to specific environmental improvements.

Box VII.8.   Important steps for support removal

- Increase the transparency of support measures;
- Prioritise support measures for removal depending on their economic and environmental inefficiencies;
- Design compensation programmes to alleviate any potential hardships caused by the support removal;
- Where possible, co-operate with other countries to achieve multilateral support reduction, but also examine unilateral support removal where net benefits will be realised as a result;
- Improve data collection and monitoring of support policies and their effects on the environment; and
- Accompany with a well-directed environmental policy.

Source: OECD (1998*d*).

For example, as mentioned in Box VII.7, after many years of subsidising the drainage of wetlands, the US government has begun a programme more recently of subsidising wetland conservation efforts instead. Similarly, under reforms of the European Union CAP, farmers are required to set-aside a set proportion of their farmlands, and are compensated for the lost income as well as for undertaking other agri-environmental measures such as the establishment of hedges or afforestation activities. Such compensation packages need to be carefully targeted, however, as shown by the Norwegian case study (Magnussen and Rymoen, 1999). Although support for leaving pastures fallow resulted in 41 per cent of farmland being set-aside in Norway in 1993, this was not as environmentally effective as had been hoped because the measures did not target the most erosion-prone lands.

The difficulties of subsidy removal should not be underestimated as recipients of subsidies will necessarily lose from such an exercise, and they are frequently politically well-organised and vocal. In many cases, however, it may be possible to design alternative programmes which better achieve the original social and economic goals of the support without the negative environmental consequences. The reform rather than removal of adverse incentives might constitute a feasible option for the conservation of biological diversity which integrates this objective into existing policies, rather than introducing it as a completely new measure.

2.   Regulations and funds – governments as guarantors of biodiversity

Governments can use direct regulatory methods to enforce or restrict certain activities which impact on biological diversity. Similarly, they can use support measures or environmental funds to actively encourage activities which promote biodiversity. Funding environmentally-friendly activities can help to close the profitability gap between these sustainable activities and any unsustainable alternatives. The use of both regulations and funds have the benefits of giving clear and easily understandable signals to all involved parties, and provide the best assurance of achieving a given level of environmental quality when there is a clear link between certain activities or emissions and their impacts on biodiversity. For example, regulations prohibiting the use of wildlife species are the most commonly used instruments to protect those in danger of extinction. The disadvantages of regulations and funds primarily arise from their financial costs (either in terms of enforcement and monitoring for regulations, or in terms of financing the environmental funds), and the inflexibility that arises from their need to specify particular activities or methods of undertaking these. As a result, they can often be economically inefficient instruments for achieving their goals.

Standards, regulations and access restrictions

Regulations enforcing or forbidding certain kinds of behaviour and access restrictions are classical administrative means to protect threatened species or biodiversity-rich natural areas. Their advantages are that they are conceptually easy to understand and that pre-formulated goals can be achieved with high probability, as long as adequate monitoring and enforcement can be assured. Most of

---

Box VII.9. Facts about regulations

Description: Legal instruments to enforce or restrict certain activities or the conditions under which they are undertaken.

Advantages: Easily understandable; legally binding; can directly target particular activities or processes.

Disadvantages: Can be an economically inefficient or costly method of achieving environmental goals, especially if proscribing certain technologies; strict enforcement necessary; inflexible; may be complex and detailed.

Applicability: Most applicable where there is a limited range of easily identifiable environmental impacts that need circumscription; and/or where the number of actors is limited.

---

the case studies examining incentives for the sustainable use or conservation of biodiversity included some regulatory or access restriction elements. This is particularly true with the creation of national parks or reserves to protect such resources, and the accompanying restrictions and regulations governing their use.

For example, managers of the Oze area in the Nikko National Park in Japan use a range of regulatory devices to protect biodiversity in the area from external pressures, primarily from visiting tourists (Planning Division, Nature Conservation Bureau, Japanese Environment Agency 1999). These include the restricted use of some areas (for example requiring visitors to use the specially constructed boardwalk, rather than walking over the marshlands), traffic restrictions during peak seasons, restrictions on the size and capacity of lodges and various voluntary measures such as 'no bathe day' and the encouragement of reduced shampoo usage. Because the pressures come primarily from large numbers of once-off visitors, clear and easy to follow regulations and restrictions on their movements and activities may be the most cost-effective means for achieving the necessary protection of the resources.

Another area suffering from tourism pressures, the coastal part of Laganas Bay on the Greek island of Zakynthos, has also relied largely on regulatory measures to protect the endangered loggerhead turtle which nests in one of the island's bays. The authorities have increasingly regulated activities that impact on the turtle's nesting grounds, including restricting building near the nesting grounds, visitor access and beach activities, fishing and marine traffic, airport operating times, and by creating a Nature Reserve in 1990 (Spyropoulou and Dimopoulos, 1999).

Given that many of the benefits of biodiversity are not privately appropriable, and that these benefits often represent significant public goods, regulations are an important tool for ensuring the conservation and sustainable use of natural resources. As they are relatively easy to design and implement, they can also be used as temporary emergency measures to secure the protection of particular aspects of biodiversity until the populations of threatened species or the integrity of the ecosystems recover to stable levels or other instruments, including raising awareness of the value of biodiversity, can be implemented to ensure the continued sustainability of the resources. Because of the restrictive nature of regulations, in the particular context of biodiversity they are instruments that are generally geared towards conservation, giving little or no consideration to sustainable use.

If carefully designed, however, they can sometimes be targeted to ensure the sustainable use of resources. For example, with the establishment of the Austrian Neusiedler See National Park (Seewinkel), various agricultural and other activities had to be prohibited (Hubacek and Bauer, 1999). It was found that some aspects of the reed industry operating in the area were not incompatible with conservation objectives. Thus, the authorities were able to allow the continued harvesting of reeds, while banning the more damaging practice of reed burning which was used to accelerate the process of reed regeneration.

Regulations and access restrictions are often used as complementary measures to other incentives, to conserve particularly sensitive ecosystems or specimens of endangered species. Thus, in addition to encouraging the generally reduced use of groundwater in the Netherlands through taxes and levies on abstraction and support to green funds, for example, there is also an intention to reduce or completely abolish groundwater abstraction in three particular zones.

The disadvantages of regulations and access restrictions are that they often impose high economic costs (inefficiencies) and are cumbersome to monitor and enforce. Thus, although the Korean people have expressed a strong preference for the conservation of the Asiatic black bear, the enforcement of the ban on hunting them is expensive, and the existing poaching and trading fines are considered to be too low compared to its trading price. As a result, at least 50 bears have been killed on Mount Chiri since 1950, leaving a total confirmed number of only six.

Similarly, it was found that a programme established in the 1970s to regulate the hunting of the big-horned in Mexico was experiencing difficulties due to poor enforcement of the regulations on the part of the government and a lack of participation of rural communities in the project (Mexican Ministry of the Environment, 1999). To counter these difficulties, the government has now designed a scheme of tradable permits for hunting rights to the sheep (see p. 81).

The high economic costs (primarily in terms of inefficiencies) of regulations and access restrictions have been examined in particular with respect to the sustainable

OECD 1999

use of fisheries. Authorities often specify a total allowable catch (TAC) and impose other gear and access restrictions to ensure the TAC is not exceeded and that sustainable harvesting methods are used. Some of the regulations go to a high degree of detail to limit fishing methods in order to maintain sustainable harvests.

It has been found that TACs encourage a race-to-fish attitude and inefficient upgrading of fishing fleet and gear. As a result, it has been recognised that TACs provide poor incentives for economic efficiency when utilised on their own, and are most effective when combined with the allocation of fishing rights to individual fishing firms (property rights), and the creation of markets for trading these rights, particularly through the distribution of individual transferable quotas (ITQs) made up of a portion of the overall TAC (see Box VII.4 above). As a final measure when other incentives and regulations have not been effective, moratoriums on over-fished fisheries can be imposed to aid in the recovery of the species.

A further problem is that while regulations and access restrictions may protect those aspects of biodiversity they are targeted towards, such as particular endangered species, they may ignore the surrounding ecosystems which can be so essential for the survival of these species. While the creation of national parks and reserves can ensure practices compatible with conservation, without suitable buffer zones they may not be sufficient. For example, the regulations in place to protect a peatland swamp in Biebrza, Poland apply almost exclusively to the areas which fall within the National Park boundaries (Polish Ministry of Environmental Protection, Natural Resources and Forestry, 1999). But the catchment of the river which feeds the peatlands extends beyond the Park boundaries, and it is significantly affected by activities outside the regulated area, particularly the abstraction of water for irrigation purposes.

A similar problem was found in the Seewinkel National Park in Austria where the import and stocking of the lake with non-native species for fishing purposes is a threat to the survival of the native species. Not only would any successful measures to stop this practice need to extend to the rest of the lake outside the park boundaries, they would also have to extend across the Austrian national borders, as part of the lake falls within Hungary. Ideally, administrative boundaries should correspond with ecosystem boundaries.

In order to overcome some of these difficulties, it is necessary to design better targeted regulations or to implement regulations in conjunction with other incentive measures. For the protection of the Asiatic black bear in Korea, simple hunting bans are combined with more innovative and effective regulations and methods of enforcing them – such as increasing poaching fines and punishments, restricting access to hiking routes during winter when bear footprints are easier to track in the snow, and hiring ex-poachers, who have the experience and the know-how to help enforce the regulations and monitor bear populations – and with other incentives such as assigning property rights to ensure that the conservation of the bears becomes more profitable for the local communities who are most able to protect them successfully. These combined measures have achieved the elimination of poaching on Mount Chiri.

Regulations are generally most useful in combination with market-based incentives, such as the assignment of well-defined property rights. In those cases, regulations can ensure that the use of biodiversity resources is indeed sustainable and contributes to the conservation of biodiversity. Given this consideration, it might not come as a surprise that no single case study has *exclusively* concentrated on regulations and access restrictions, but that *all* case studies have included a regulatory component in their mix of incentive measures.

Environmental funds and public financing

Most of the case studies found that there was some sort of public financing available for biodiversity conservation, and some of them focused entirely on environmental funds set up for this purpose. Because of the various difficulties discussed above in designing economic instruments to internalise the costs of biodiversity loss, and the enforcement and monitoring costs of regulations and access restrictions, many governments prefer to utilise "positive incentives" to encourage the sustainable use and conservation of biodiversity, rather than punishing or discouraging the activities that lead to biodiversity loss. These "positive incentives" work by providing monetary payments, tax reductions or other financial incentives either for conservation or restoration activities, or for the inducement of sustainable behaviour from the users of the biodiverse resources, closing the profitability gap between sustainable practices and their unsustainable alternatives. They generally take the form of either specially designed environmental funds or support measures ranging from the provision of infrastructure without cost recuperation to tax exemptions for biodiversity-friendly activities.[30]

Environmental funds

The establishment of dedicated funds for the conservation and the sustainable use of biodiversity is an instrument that enjoys growing popularity in OECD and non-OECD countries alike.[31] Where government supported, these funds are either financed by a lump sum from general tax receipts, from one-off receipts such as proceeds from the sale of state assets or from dedicated charges or fees (see above). While environmental funds are not firmly grounded in economic theory – which maintains that worthwhile activities should be financed out of general tax receipts in order to avoid economic inefficiencies – the visibility and transparency of the work of such funds has made them attractive in the eyes of policy makers as well as

---

Box VII.10. Facts about environmental funds

Description:	Revenue or resources that are set-aside or earmarked for specific environmental purposes; may be from public or private sources.
Advantages:	Transparent and high visibility; positive public relations.
Disadvantages:	May not maximise economic efficiency; may be inflexible because use of the funds are earmarked to some extent.
Applicability:	Where governments have difficulties raising general funds; where fiscal infrastructure is weak; and where clearly identifiable and highly popular causes exist.

---

to the general public which can support their work with the help of private donations.

The "earmarking" of government funds for particular projects or activities has advantages and disadvantages. Largely these depend on how narrowly defined the earmarking is. Some degree of earmarking is the identifying characteristic of an environmental fund, because otherwise these funds would simply form part of general government expenditures. If the activities financed by the earmarked funds are too broadly defined, however, the advantages of public communication of the issues and the creation of support around a popular topic might be lost. If it is too narrowly defined, on the other hand, the money may not be able to be fully spent and the specified activities may not be the best option either environmentally or from an economic efficiency perspective.

Perhaps the best solution is to ensure strict and transparent processes in the allocation and disbursement of the funds. As discussed in Section VI.2 above, the use of public review and advice processes – such as through advisory councils or public hearings – can ensure relevance and transparency in the decision-making process. Ideally, there should be a high degree of flexibility in the allocation of the funds, but situated within a broader, generally agreed upon, context. An examination of the case studies indicates the variations available in the design, operation and financing of such environmental funds. For example, in order to help in the sustainable management of Oze National Park, a trust fund – the Oze Conservation Fund – was established. This Fund operates under a budget of 1.4 billion yen p.a. (approximately US$ 10 million by 1998 exchange rate), half of which comes from public sources and half from private donations. The Fund is used to undertake educational and institutional building work, as well as management decisions regarding the Park. In Poland, where there are limited public funds available internally for

95

nature conservation and a dedicated environmental fund, there is instead an active debt-for-nature EcoFund which allows Polish debt to other countries to be traded against the contribution of funds to environmental projects (OECD, 1998e).

Environmental funds are often designed to compensate land owners who are no longer allowed to undertake certain activities on their lands. Thus, in New Zealand, the Forest Heritage Fund was created in 1990 to compensate those private forest owners who are no longer allowed to log sections of their land (Hutching, 1999). In the United Kingdom, in addition to the payments made to private land managers to conserve heathlands under the EU Agri-Environmental Regulations, support is also given in the form of environmental funds (Harley and Davies, 1999). The recently introduced landfill tax there allows for the crediting of up to 20 per cent of the tax revenues collected by landfill operators to approved environmental funds. Under this scheme, there are at least three projects that have been approved so far for the Dorset heathlands. Similarly, a portion of the receipts from the UK national lottery are given to a heritage fund, which will be spending £14 million on heathland management schemes in Cornwall, Suffolk and Shropshire over the next five years, under a project led by English Nature.

In Australia, the innovative Revolving Fund for Nature was set up to finance purchases by the Trust for Nature Victoria (TNV) of ecologically sensitive lands. Once land is purchased, TNV draws up a legally-binding covenant specifying the necessary restrictions and conservation activities required to maintain the habitat, and resells the land to owners whose use of the land will be bound by the specifications in the covenant. Although this sometimes requires reselling the land at a lower price than it was originally purchased for by the Fund, a significant portion of the original capital is still available for the purchase of other lands for similar treatment. Thus the Fund, de facto, finances the *incremental* costs between sustainable and unsustainable activities.

Because they provide a high profile political platform for the conservation of biodiversity in a transparent manner, such funds are often preferred by the public. For example, 60 per cent of those surveyed about conservation efforts in the Garonne Valley in France stated that they would prefer to contribute to a dedicated environmental fund than to a general increase in local taxes which would be used to finance equivalent conservation measures (Amigues and Desaigues, 1999). It was found that there was a general mistrust of the disbursement of unspecified government finances, and the public felt more comfortable with a transparent and dedicated fund.

Public financing

Many countries also employ specifically targeted support measures – financed from general government receipts – to reduce the costs of undertaking activities in

---

Box VII.11. Facts about public financing

Description: Government support that is given to encourage or enable biodiversity conserving activities.

Advantages: Popular with recipients; promotes desirable activities, rather than prohibiting undesirable ones.

Disadvantages: Requires funding; may lead to economic inefficiencies; may encourage rent-seeking behaviour.

Applicability: Applicable in situations where a desirable activity would not be undertaken without support; or to create a differential in favour of such activities when it is not feasible to discourage the undesirable alternatives.

---

an environmentally sustainable manner. These can take the form of direct payments for environmental activities, tax exemptions or reductions, subsidies to environmentally preferred inputs or equipment, or the provision of infrastructure necessary for the sustainable use of resources.

As mentioned on p. 87 above, many of the often significant subsidies to agriculture in OECD countries are now being reformed to link them to the undertaking of specific environmental activities. Thus, one of the case studies (Hoppichler and Groier, 1999) found that the reform of Austrian agricultural subsidies in the second half of the 1980s and early 1990s led to a greater emphasis on the agri-ecological aspects of funding and an integration of environment related direct payments into the funding system. These reforms were implemented according to EU Regulation 2078/92, which defines the nature and amount of agri-environmental payments that can be paid to farmers under the reformed Common Agricultural Policy. A number of environmentally-beneficial changes in the Austrian agricultural sector have resulted from the subsidy reforms, including a declining use of pesticides and fertilisers, increased use of integrated management systems, the expansion of crop rotation systems, and significant growth in the number of organic farms.

The use of tax expenditures (either reductions or exemptions) to encourage sustainable activities are particularly effective when those who undertake the biodiversity-threatening activities are presented with two or more options for carrying out the activities, one of which is significantly preferable from an environmental perspective. By reducing or exempting the tax rates associated with the environmentally preferred activity, while leaving them at their original level for the alternative options, the government sends a clear message which activity they wish

---

Box VII.12.   Tax exemptions for green funds

Since 1995, the Dutch government has offered tax exemptions to individuals who invest in approved green investment funds.[32] Interest and dividend derived from the green funds are exempt from income tax, thus allowing investors in green projects to contract loans at reduced interest rates (usually about 2 per cent less than commercial interest rates) and providing a positive incentive to invest in green funds rather than standard investment funds. Even with this tax exemption, it was found that the green investment funds still have a lower rate of return than some other funds. Despite this, they have been heavily supported by the Dutch people, with most banks currently operating at least one green investment fund and more money invested in green funds than can actually be utilised in the available schemes.

Source: Bellegem *et al.* (1999*b*).

---

to encourage. If set correctly, these tax reductions can create a pricing differential between the activities, such that the preferred activity becomes more economically attractive than the less-preferred alternatives. In addition, the case studies of the green investment funds in the Netherlands found that such tax exemptions and the "feel good" factor of undertaking more environmentally beneficial activities can encourage the preferred activities even when they remain more costly than the alternatives (see Box VII.12).

In another example, the National Task Force on Economic Instruments and Disincentives to Sound Environmental Practices in Canada deliberated in 1994 on incentives and disincentives in the taxation system with regard to biodiversity conservation. Their final recommendations included amending the *Canadian Income Tax Act* to exempt from capital gains tax all donations or conservation covenants of ecologically sensitive lands made in perpetuity to all levels of government and charities (Rubec, 1999).

Many governments also provide some of the infrastructure necessary for the sustainable use of biodiverse resources. Thus, in the Oze National Park in Japan, authorities have provided special toilets, waste water treatment infrastructure and a wooden boardwalk over the sensitive marshlands in order to reduce the impacts of the many tourists on the Park environment. In the Biebrza National Park in Poland, a project is being planned to speed up the silting over of three big channels constructed through the peatlands in the Park. In addition to the provision of infrastructure to reduce the impacts of human activities on biodiversity, some govern-ments also provide infrastructure for the immediate protection or benefit of particular species. Thus, on the island of Zakynthos, in addition to upgrading tourist facilities to make them more environmentally-friendly, authorities have also pro-tected the threatened turtles through installing metal nesting cages for them on the beaches. Similarly, in the Mount Chiri National Park in Korea, an eco-corridor is under construction to connect divided habitats to allow the better movement of wild animals, including the Asiatic black bear, around the mountain.

As with environmental funds, direct subsidies are often used to compensate those whose activities are restricted according to biodiversity management plans. For example, in the Seewinkel Park in Austria, a range of compensation packages are offered to those affected by the restrictions imposed by the creation of the Park. Landowners who cede their land to the National Park are compensated, as are licensed hunters who are no longer able to hunt in the grounds. If a policy is devel-oped to cease the import and stocking of the lake with non-native fish, the affected fishers will also be compensated. Similarly, subsidies are sometimes used to com-pensate agricultural producers or fishermen for restricted use of these resources through, for example, land set-aside schemes or vessel buy-back programmes.

3. The importance of context – framework building as an incentive measure

No incentive measure is implemented in a vacuum. The political context, the form and functionality of institutions, the degree of information available, and the stakeholders involved all influence the effectiveness of incentive measures for the conservation and the sustainable use of biodiversity. However, one might ask if these framework conditions constitute incentive measures in their own right.

The correct answer is: they can be, depending on the characteristics of the problem which the incentive measures are required to address. In order to clarify this distinction – and proceeding from the idea discussed in the preceding chapter that the loss of biodiversity constitutes a market failure – it is necessary to ask "why do markets fail?", or "why do markets for the values of biological diversity not exist?". The answer provided by the economist Ronald Coase was: transaction costs.[33]

This argument that the continued existence of externalities is due to transac-tion costs has led some people to conclude that the *status quo* is actually optimal: the loss of biodiversity does constitute a loss, but overcoming the transaction costs will be even more expensive or it would already have been done. This argument fails to see that in a dynamic policy context, it is the task of public policy to increase social welfare by providing the necessary information and institutions that lower these transaction costs. Also, a number of the case studies in which valuation techniques

---

Box VII.13.   The free-rider problem and the "tragedy of the commons"

Problems of externalities and public goods are sometimes also referred to as "free-rider problems" or the "tragedy of the commons".[34] Free-riders participate in the benefits of public goods, such as biological diversity, but do not participate in the costs of maintaining or restoring them. If the public good is being consumed during use, free-riding leads to rapid degradation and depletion of the public goods. If public goods are costly to provide, free-riding leads to less provision of public goods than would be ideal.

The problem of free-riding frequently arises in situations where well-defined property rights, of the private or the public kind, are absent and a valuable resource, say a forest or a fishery, is accessible to everyone. In this situation everyone is a free-rider, as nobody feels responsible for limiting use and/or restoration. In the absence of appropriate incentive measures, rapid depletion and eventual disappearance are the consequence.

---

were used to estimate the social value of biodiversity conservation generally found that these estimates far outweighed the costs of implementing the necessary measures to achieve that conservation.[35]

Policy makers also have at their disposal a series of means to *lower* transaction costs for private actors that make decisions which either threaten or conserve biodiversity, *i.e.* by generating and transmitting the relevant information, as well as defining and enforcing rights and liabilities. Once the transaction costs are permanently lowered in this way, private actors can again bargain between themselves to arrive at new outcomes which increase total societal welfare. In this sense, the lowering of transaction costs through information provision and institution-building acts in itself as an incentive measure that policy makers can chose to utilise or not.

Of course, information and institutions play a greater role in some policy contexts than in others. For example, when considering the health impacts of environmental pollution, reasonably precise measurements concerning morbidity and mortality will allow in many cases the formulation of adequate minimum standards. In addition, once the relevant information has been gathered, it is unlikely to change dramatically through time.

The situation is more difficult with respect to biological diversity. While many agree on the policy-relevance of biodiversity loss, the individual parameters of the problem which could become the basis for the definition of economic incentive measures are ill-defined. Conceptual controversies make the generation of widely-accepted "correct" information about biodiversity values or the costs associated with its loss a significant problem. Not only are there different ecosystems, species, and genetic resources to be considered, but 'hot spot' approaches compete with general policy integration, the inefficient rent dissipation of natural assets with private values is confused with true public good problems, and issues of conservation are complicated by their links to other policy areas such as those of development and trade.

In order to counter the important market, informational and institutional failures that result in the inefficient loss of biodiversity, these controversial questions need to be addressed and some means of providing generally acceptable information and building adequate institutions for monitoring and enforcing the sustainable use and conservation of biodiversity are necessary and require initial investments by public authorities.

The finding of a common language and the exchange of views between stakeholders are as important in these contexts as any single, traditional incentive measure. A particularly important role is the education of, and provision of information to, policy makers and administrators in order to ensure the appropriate policy actions are taken to prevent biodiversity loss. While it is true that biodiversity policy is in the relatively early stages of development and that, after a time of study and consultation, traditional economic incentives aimed at static optimisation may be able to solve the problems, the complex and dynamic nature of biodiversity makes this state of affairs unlikely. Of course, these considerations do not constitute arguments *against* the use of economic instruments as presented in Section 1 of this chapter or regulations and funds as presented in Section 2, they only present arguments *for* the combination of these instruments with others which reflect some of the basic informational and institutional necessities of the problem.

Information provision and scientific and technical capacity building

The loss of biological diversity can be interpreted in many cases as the non-realisation of its true value. While the non-realisation of its true value can be due to the lack of formal incentive measures for its protection, say charges or regulations, the absence of appropriate information can also be the underlying reason itself for this lack of incentive measures. It has been emphasised above that achieving full information concerning the functions and the value of biodiversity is an illusory goal. Nevertheless, the provision of information about the services of biodiversity, and their economic measurement in particular, can galvanise public opinion, mobilise political support and contribute to the formulation of appropriate incentive measures.

In this sense, information provision can be understood as an incentive measure in its own right, as was shown by the Canadian study which re-examined the decision to build a reservoir once calculations had been made of the monetary

---

Box VII.14. Facts about information provision as incentive measure

Description: Ensuring scientific and technological information is at the disposal of decision-makers and stakeholders.

Advantages: Indispensable basis for objective decision-making.

Disadvantages: Costly; will on its own not suffice as an incentive measure for the provision of public goods.

Applicability: Applicable for the large number of situations in biodiversity policy-making which are characterised by uncertainty and ignorance.

---

costs and benefits of the environmental impacts of the reservoir. As discussed in Section III.1 above, once these values were included in the original benefit-cost estimates, it became clear that the construction of the reservoir would lead to a net loss in economic welfare of approximately CAN$ 10 million. As these values were not calculated when the original decision was taken, the project went ahead at a loss to wider social welfare.

The Norwegian case study made a similar valuation, this time of the benefits of the water quality, recreation and biodiversity aspects associated with watercourses there. This information was found to be particularly useful in informing expert panel meetings of political and administrative personnel in the relevant areas as part of a programme to increase awareness and design appropriate conservation measures for the watercourses. As part of this project, focus groups of local residents were organised, and a survey about the value of the watercourses was taken – all of which contributed to increasing local knowledge of the issues and encouraging stakeholder involvement. These, and many of the other country case studies, highlighted the large information failures that exist with respect to the public goods of biodiversity, and how information provision can lead to decisive improvements in policy performance.

One of the studies from the Netherlands on green investment funds (Bellegem *et al.*, 1999*a*) found that a lack of scientific knowledge and public awareness of the effects of groundwater abstraction on local ecologies not only hampered the implementation of appropriate incentive measures, but was also used as an excuse to not take any action at all. On the brighter side, the US case study on wetlands management emphasised how once scientific knowledge and public awareness of the value of biodiversity have been established – as they had by the late 1960s for wetlands in the US – public policy can respond quickly and effectively to implement appropriate conservation measures.

The building and sharing of scientific knowledge of the effects of different pressures on biodiversity thus represents an essential step in the development of policies to conserve or sustainably use natural resources. In recent years, a vast amount of information has been compiled on the properties and functions of Earth's living organisms. Biodiversity databases exist which range from those that indicate the distribution of plants, animals and microbes around the globe, to detailed genomic maps, to compilations of the physiological functions of organisms, to information about the behaviour and function of individual species within ecosystems (see Box VII.15). These databases are now increasingly drawn upon by policy makers in need of information.

Because such data has often been collected through independent and unrelated projects, their full economic, scientific and political potential have not been realised. There is today a pressing need for software tools and standards for accessing, linking and correlating these disparate databases, and for co-ordination among database developers, owners and users. Joint international efforts can create new applications and opportunities for using this information resource in public policy, economic development and scientific research, thus strengthening the utilisation and conservation of biodiversity resources. In addition, one key element needed to link these disparate databases – an electronic catalogue containing the correct scientific names of the earth's named species – needs to be completed.

The OECD Megascience Forum has concluded that governments can play a leading role in enhancing the usefulness of biological databases by establishing an international co-ordinating body, and a new distributed, linked, modular information network that would allow users to navigate the vast quantities of biodiversity data. This network would incorporate intelligent specialised search and analysis tools for supporting research and decision-making in areas such as health, environmental protection, agriculture, and education. Acting together, governments will also be able to accelerate the compilation of data about living organisms, especially those whose existence is threatened. The additional cost for all of these activities will be modest compared with the amounts currently being spent on biological databases

Of course, the generation and communication of the relevant information requires the existence of experts, researchers and communicators with appropriate capabilities and competencies. As a result, both the Dorset Heathlands Project in England and the Australian Revolving Fund for Nature use their accumulated knowledge and skills about conservation and sustainable use of biodiverse ecologies not only directly in the implementation of relevant conservation projects, but also to advise and provide training for other organisations and individuals. The case study about the Revolving Fund notes that, given the lack of information on species and ecological processes, and the dearth of economic studies on biodiversity loss in Australia, such capacity building is a particularly important tool for preventing further biodiversity loss.

103

Box VII.15.   Some international biodiversity databases

- The Clearing House Mechanism (CHM) is an international initiative supporting the Convention on Biological Diversity by promoting and facilitating technical and scientific co-operation between countries. It is intended to provide global access to and exchange of information on biological diversity and its sustainable use (see http://www.biodiv.org).
- The World Conservation Monitoring Centre (WCMC) was set-up by the IUCN, WWF and UNEP to provide information services on conservation and sustainable use of the world's living resources and to help others to develop information systems of their own (see http://www.wcmc.org.uk).
- The EVRI facility discussed above is an example of an internet-based database of economic valuation studies of different aspects of biodiversity for use in conducting economic valuation studies through benefits transfers (see http://www.evri.ec.gc.ca).
- Twelve international organisations and networks have also collaborated to form the Biodiversity Conservation Information System (BCIS) to ensure the co-operative provision of data, information, advice and related services to support environmentally sound decision-making and action with respect to biodiversity and landscapes (see http://www.biodiversity.org).

Also the design, implementation, monitoring and enforcement of incentive measures requires specific sets of skills at all levels. An issue which is closely linked to and sometimes identical with the building of capacity is education of the general public, as well as of policy makers and administrators dealing with biological diversity. Education and capacity building ensure that abstractly designed incentives are not taken from a shelf but can be adapted to yield real benefits for the conservation and the sustainable use of biodiversity.

Many of the national parks discussed in the studies (including ones in Poland, Japan, and Greece) used a range of interactive and educational devices for increasing local community and the public's knowledge of biodiversity and its values. These ranged from local education centres and educational paths with points of interest marked, to the employment and training of local wardens to protect turtle nests on Zakynthos Island and the implementation of awareness raising schemes such as the "trash carry home programme" and "voluntary no bathe day" in the Oze National Park in Japan.

The community forestry development project in Turkey has realised the necessity of active community involvement in efforts to reduce biodiversity loss and other negative environmental effects of unsustainable forestry practices, and has developed an extensive *in situ* practical training programme for forest villagers. The next stage there is to extend education on the integrated relationship between up and downstream activities. By developing the link between income generation and sustainable management of the forest, and by giving the villagers the knowledge-based tools to achieve this, the education programme provides a substantial incentive for reducing biodiversity loss.

A particularly important issue is the implementation of certification and eco-labelling schemes which not only increase awareness of biodiversity issues, but also provide a vehicle for consumers to directly influence the level of sustainable activities. On this basis, Finland has designed a voluntary forest certification scheme which will be operational from 1998 and is compatible with international certification schemes. Despite the fact that there has been little scientific research into forest values, forest conservation is a high priority for the Finnish people and as such many farmers and forest owners have preserved small forest areas on their own initiative. The use of a certification scheme will allow wood-product consumers from both Finland and international markets the choice of purchasing products they know have been made from sustainably harvested wood. The case study on organic farming in the Netherlands also highlighted the public education aspects of eco-labelling of organic produce, as well as the marketing benefits of access to green and local markets.

As part of the educational and capacity building process, particular species or areas have often become identified with biodiversity conservation efforts. While the use of the panda bear as the logo for the World Wildlife Fund (WWF) is widely familiar, particular nations or regions often adopt a local species or park as representative of national conservation programmes. For example, bears are probably the most important national symbol for the Korean people, with local legend maintaining that the first Koreans arose from the mating of the son of a god and a woman who was transformed from an Asiatic black bear after 100 days of avoiding the sun and eating only mugwort and garlic. As a result, the extremely endangered Asiatic black bear – which currently survives only at Mount Chiri in South Korea and in the demilitarised zone between North and South Korea – was designated as a national monument in 1982, thus increasing awareness and facilitating policy efforts.

Similarly, in Greece the endangered loggerhead sea turtle has become a flag-species for coastal biodiversity conservation, with information and awareness campaigns increasing knowledge not only about this species, but about the sustainable use of coastal zones in general.

Some countries have also developed conservation campaigns around certain well known or popular bio-diverse regions. For example, the Oze National Park in Japan is valued as a national "treasure", not only for its scenic beauty, but also for its

---

Box VII.16. Conservation of keystone species

While generally the conservation of particular species will be best conducted within an overall programme to conserve the ecosystem which constitutes the habitat of the threatened species, measures directly targeting the physical conservation or sustainable use of a particular species can sometimes be essential for its continued existence, or may prove either sufficient to address the problem independently or complementary to other general ecosystem approaches. In addition, it may be easier to galvanise support for biodiversity conservation measures around the protection of a particular keystone species because it is easier to communicate and understand than the conservation of the surrounding ecosystem.

There are three types of physical measures that can be used to protect individual members of a threatened species where such protection is desirable, and preferably within an overall programme to sustain the surrounding ecosystem:

- restricting access or use of the species or its supporting habitat, through limits or total prohibitions on harvesting or trade in the species (for example, under the Convention on International Trade in Endangered Species, CITES), or the creation of limited access parks or reserves;

- physically enhancing the habitat of the species, including the provision of food or protection (such as the metal nesting cages provided for the sea turtles in Greece), or the provision of movement tunnels or corridors to connect separated habitat zones; and

- as a last resort, the transfer of surviving members of the threatened species to safer habitats or to protected breeding programmes.

These measures are best combined with the raising of awareness about the pressures on the species, the provision of compensation or other incentives to the relevant parties to cease exerting these pressures, and adequate enforcement and monitoring procedures. Some of these measures can be extremely expensive, and are generally only used when a species is under severe threat or is endangered.

---

tradition for conservation. It became known across the country through a popular song about Oze in 1949 and later through the widely publicised struggle of a local man, now considered a "national hero", who successfully appealed plans in the 1970s to construct a national road through the Park. The resulting public awareness has not only made Oze a popular tourist destination, it has also facilitated awareness raising across the country about conservation efforts in general. The creation of widely recognisable symbolic representations reflect popular cultural and regional identities, and can serve as important communication tools in efforts to reduce biodiversity loss.

Economic valuation as incentive measure and support for decision-making

It is possible to employ a broad range of implicit and explicit, quantitative and qualitative evaluation methods for biodiversity policy decision-making. These may include economic (monetary) evaluation methods for cost-benefit analysis, as well as other evaluation methods based either on qualitative criteria (*e.g.* voting) or on informational or institutional performance criteria of economic activities (*e.g.* disclosure, labelling, stakeholder involvement, benefit sharing).

Box VII.17.   Facts about economic valuation of biodiversity

Description: Determines monetary values for environmental goods and services for which market values do not exist.

Advantages: Provides important information for decision-making based on the benefits of biodiversity conservation.

Disadvantages: Can be costly to undertake; the results are difficult to communicate; the derived monetary values are often open to challenge; expertise is not always available.

Applicability: Where widely accepted values for the non-market environmental goods and services exist; where decisions will otherwise be taken on the basis of economic valuations with a zero value for environmental effects.

Such analyses are commonly used as the basis for policy decisions already, although they have often been under-utilised for environmental purposes because so many environmental goods and services are difficult to quantify or compare qualitatively, and providing monetary estimates of their benefits and costs can be contentious. However, strong progress has been made in recent years to develop appropriate methodologies to overcome these problems, and economic valuation of the full costs and benefits of projects is now frequently used as an important tool for informing decision-makers. In fact, the Fourth Conference of Parties to the Convention on Biological Diversity in May 1998 specifically recognised that "economic valuation of biodiversity and biological resources is an important tool for well-targeted and calibrated economic incentive measures" (Decision IV/10).

In principle, a full evaluation of the complete range of biodiversity benefits in a given situation should cover all or most aspects of the natural resources of the ecosystem, including their:

- use values;

- amenity values;

- ecosystem services (*e.g.* flood control, water purification, soil maintenance);

- existence, cultural and ethical values; and

- option and quasi-option values.

In practice, this is not so easy to accomplish. As was found in the Norwegian study, "biodiversity in general is difficult to value. The case studies [for that project] therefore did not aim at valuing "biological diversity" as such" (*cf.* 10). Instead, these studies examined specific local aspects of biodiversity, particularly relating to changes (improvements) in the quality of easily identifiable aspects of local biodiversity.

Box VII.18. Environmental valuation techniques

A range of techniques can be used to determine economic values for biodiversity goods and services, including:

- **methods based on actual market prices** – employ existing information on market prices from actual transactions relating to the environmental goods and services. These techniques include examining actual expenditures, changes in productivity, the market price of output, and using appraisals.

- **methods based on surrogate market prices** – indirectly uses information on market prices as a proxy to estimate benefits from environmental goods and services. These techniques include travel cost method, expenditure-based methods, hedonic pricing methods, property value methods and replacement cost methods.

- **methods based on simulated market prices** – methods used when little or no actual market information exists. Involve administering a sample survey of a population to gather data on their willingness-to-pay (WTP) for an environmental good or service or their willingness-to-accept (WTA) payment for the loss of such a good or service. These 'stated preference' techniques include contingent valuation methods, cashless choice method and contingent ranking.

Source: Filion and Adamowicz (1994).

As mentioned above, the Canadian case study found that when estimates of the costs of biodiversity loss associated with a reservoir development were taken into consideration, there was a net loss of just over CAN$ 10 million from the overall project. Because these external costs were not calculated for the original decision to construct the reservoir, it was deemed to have greater benefits than costs associated with it and the project went ahead. When the non-market environmental costs were eventually estimated through the transfer of estimates from other contingent valuation and travel-cost method studies (using a benefits transfer procedure – see Box VII.19), it was found that they amounted to a significant portion (14-16 per cent) of the total costs of the project. Such an evaluation constitutes in itself an incentive measure, as it allows biodiversity values to be explicitly integrated into the policy process necessary to overcome market failures.

The French and Norwegian case studies used valuation techniques to estimate the benefits of biodiversity conservation in particular areas. In the French case, the benefits and costs of a hypothetical biodiversity conservation programme in the Garonne Valley were compared. Contingent valuation studies were used to determine what farmers with riparian lands were willing to accept in compensation for implementing biodiversity conservation programmes on the land bordering the river, and what the public was willing to pay them to do so. It was found that the amount the public was willing to pay over a five year period would cover the payments to farmers according to their stated willingness to accept for a twenty-five year period of conservation.[36]

In the Norwegian study, economic valuations were conducted of the benefits associated with conservation or improvements to environmental quality in two Norwegian water courses. Contingent valuation studies were again used to survey benefit components connected to different user and conservation interests associated with the watercourses. The valuation study in this case was seen as the first important step in implementing incentive measures. In addition to eliciting the necessary information to make an informed decision about the proposed conservation programmes, the survey and the follow-up meetings to discuss its results also provided an important source of information for local inhabitants about the pressures on the water courses and the possible conservation programmes that could be undertaken.

The Korean case study also used a contingent valuation survey to estimate the willingness-to-pay of the Korean people for the preservation of the Asiatic black bear. It was estimated that they would be willing to pay an amazing US$ 380.6 million per bear for their preservation. The majority of this was attributed to the preservation value of the species, while only US$ 71.5 million was for actual "use" of the bear through scientific or non-consumptive activities. Given that the market value of a poached bear is approximately US$ 67-133 thousand, each poaching was estimated to cost the nation's social welfare at least US$ 257 million, representing a considerable negative externality.

This study indicates that if the social costs of the biodiversity loss were imputed into the costs of harvesting the bears, the revenue the poachers would

> ### Box VII.19.   Benefits transfer as an alternative to primary valuation studies
>
> Benefits transfer is an approach that uses economic values estimated in previous valuations studies and applies them to a decision maker's current policy and programme needs. The main advantage of benefits transfers is that they can require significantly less time and financial resources to derive value estimates as compared with primary valuation efforts. In addition to being utilised where resources are limited, benefits transfers may be useful in policy contexts where "rough and crude" benefits estimates may be used as a screening device for evaluating the worth of a policy or project. The Environmental Valuation Reference Inventory (see Box VI.2 above) is a promising new tool that has been designed specifically for this purpose.
>
> While there are definite advantages to using benefits transfer approaches in some circumstances, analysts must recognise that their results can only be as accurate as the primary study estimates themselves and their similarities to these benefits. In addition, there are a number of challenges associated with successful and defensible benefit transfers, including the specification of the environmental good or service or human health effect under examination; locating relevant studies; assessing the suitability and quality of the study to be transferred; and the actual transfer of the values to the new study.
>
> _____
>
> *Sources*:   OECD (1994); De Civita *et al.* (1998); and Brookshire and Neil (1992).

receive would be significantly less than their costs. Developing mechanisms to transfer some of these social costs to the poachers would ideally result in a cessation of the bear poaching. However, because they are already operating outside of legal markets, it is nearly impossible to apply market-based incentives such as fees, charges or taxes to such operations. Instead, information provision and stricter regulatory instruments (with appropriate enforcement) are likely to be the most useful tools until such time as the bear population recovers to sustainable levels, and then the use of a system of sustainable harvesting may be possible.

While economic valuations of the full benefits and costs of biodiversity conservation can both ensure that decision-making processes are better informed and constitute a useful tool in the education of the public and the involvement of stakeholders in these processes, there are qualifications to such studies. Some of the common problems include survey biases that arise from data aggregation over large populations or regions; a lack of awareness about budget constraints on willingness to accept surveys; 'anchoring biases' that occur with close-ended questionnaires which put an upper or lower limit on the acceptable willingness to pay or accept; the true values for the good or service under question can be embedded in a wider environmental good than the survey specifies (as was the case with the French and Korean studies); a "warm-glow effect" may lead to an overestimation of goods when those surveyed declare what they would usually give as "gifts" to the environmental causes in question; social, cultural and environmental values of a qualitative nature also have to be explicitly and separately considered in the policy making process, not just those benefits and costs for which monetary values are established; and economic valuation studies have to be complemented as appropriate by definition, explanation, communication and capacity building.

Many of these criticisms apply to all forms of human understanding and attempts to transform a complex reality into neat, easily understandable concepts. For instance, the scientific assessment of biodiversity also faces huge difficulties, as does the appraisal of the social and the political implications. But the economic valuation of biodiversity is faced with the principal problem of trying to express the value of goods which (not without reason) have previously been unpriced in monetary terms. The continuing tension between the ever more sophisticated attempts to quantify the monetary values of biodiversity goods and services and the difficulties such projects face has to be approached by all sides with an open mind and in a pragmatic perspective in order to realise the benefits that the monetary evaluation of biodiversity can bring.

Because of these theoretical and practical difficulties, economic valuation based on contingent valuation is frequently resisted on principal grounds precisely by those parties most interested in the conservation of biodiversity, such as environmental NGOs. As a result, there has been an increasing shift from the establishment of monetary values for the more difficult to conceptualise attributes of biodiversity – such as its existence value – and towards the more readily definable and quantifiable attributes of ecosystem services such as flood control, air and water purification.

The task for the policy maker is here to build bridges between the proponents and the detractors of economic valuation by identifying in which cases economic valuation can be pragmatically used and in which cases alternative, implicit methods of valuation (e.g. discussion or voting) should be used instead. Claims of unlimited applicability, as much as apprehension about its results built on poorly qualified general objections, can limit the contribution of economic valuation towards progress in the successful implementation of incentive measures. While it is true that economic valuations of biodiversity values can be complex and contentious, they also play a strategic role in the development of incentives for biodiversity conservation or sustainable use, and as such should be encouraged and the methodologies for undertaking such valuations developed further.

OECD 1999

Institution building and stakeholder involvement

As has been emphasised above, the generation, processing and dissemination of relevant information is in itself an important element in the design of policies for the conservation and the sustainable use of biological diversity. In order to be effectively communicated or combined with other sorts of relevant information such as political assessments or stakeholder opinions, this information needs to be channelled through the appropriate institutions.

Box VII.20. Facts about institution building

Description: Creation or strengthening of specifically designed institutions for biodiversity management.

Advantages: Assembly of competencies and representation of multiple stake-holders necessary to manage complex situations with overlapping concerns.

Disadvantages: High set-up costs; might add to bureaucracy if competencies and capacity is not clearly allocated.

Applicability: Considerations of appropriate institutions apply to all situations in which biodiversity is under pressure.

Institutions mediate the creation and implementation of incentive measures and also monitor, enforce and assess them. Without the necessary institutions, it is difficult or even impossible to design or implement the necessary measures for biodiversity conservation. For instance, the case study on the Biebrza National Park and State Forests found that an adequate legal and regulatory framework for reclaiming or protecting peatlands was severely lacking, making it very difficult to effectively counter the threats to sustainable peatland management. This study recommended the development of a unified spatial management plan for the whole area, to overcome the confusion and difficulties associated with the relevant responsibilities being shared by different levels and types of government.

In some cases, suitable institutions already exist, but may have to be adapted for specific biodiversity-related problems. Sometimes, this can be a more difficult task than forming new institutions. For example, in the Netherlands there are a number of traditional and non-representational water drainage organisations (Bellegem et al., 1999a). Because for many years the water table in the country was too high, water drainage policies were extremely important for conserving the environment. However, now that the excessive abstraction of ground water has led to desiccation and a concomitant loss of biodiversity, these water drainage organisations need to be reformed to represent the changing needs of nature conservation in the country.

There can also be difficulties and confusion when more than one institution is responsible for different aspects of the management of a single biodiversity resource requiring protection. This was seen in the Polish study as discussed above, and used to be the case also in Korea in connection with the conservation of the black bear in Mount Chiri National Park. In Korea, the Ministry of Culture and Sports was responsible for the protection of national monuments (including the bear since 1982); the Ministry of Home Affairs managed the National Parks, including Mount Chiri where the bear lives; the Forestry Administration managed the forests, mammals and birds on the mountain; and the overall responsibility for nature conservation was under the direction of the Ministry of the Environment. Due to the decentralised nature of these functions, the Government lacked in the past the ability to respond systematically to the pressures threatening species or ecosystems. Since February 1998, however, the Ministry of the Environment is solely responsible for all aspects of the management of the natural park, a development which should help to consolidate the achievements in suppressing the poaching of the bear.

In other cases, institutions have to be newly created to address the problems of biodiversity loss. It can be assumed that general policy making institutions are adequately established in most OECD Member countries. However, biodiversity policy poses special challenges. Several case studies refer to newly established panels, administrations and processes for the achievement of better policy results. For example, a Trust Fund (including but not limited to the financing of conservation measures) was established in 1995 for the management of Oze National Park in Japan, under the auspices of the Oze Conservation Foundation. The Fund represents an institutional collaboration of public and private interests, local people, environmentalists, and scientists who undertake promotional and advocational functions and support the activities of government or other private bodies. Stakeholder participation in these decisions, from both local and national interests, has been strong and other parks are currently trying to adopt a similar institutional framework.

In order to gain the co-operation of all relevant parties in the Finnish voluntary certification scheme, and to fully utilise the knowledge of the various parties, a broad-based group which includes environmental organisations, farmers, and others was formed in 1996 to design the certification scheme. The Danish scheme for transforming privately cultivated forest areas into strict forest reserves also emphasised the importance that the scheme be both voluntary and compensated in order to get the full co-operation of the private land owners.

Formal and informal institutions also organise the involvement of stakeholders. The involvement of local populations only arises as separate issues in the implementation of incentive measures because there exist groups of people who are affected by biodiversity-related policy and who are crucial for its success, but which do not *automatically* participate in the formulation of policy. In order to build the trust and gain the co-operation of stakeholders in the policies responsible for biodiversity protection, it is essential that measures are predictable, clearly understandable, and achieve their stated objectives.

In some instances, it has been found that non-government institutions are better able to garner local support and stakeholder involvement than government institutions. This can stem from a general lack of trust in the efficiency and effectiveness of some public sector activities. Thus, the Revolving Fund for biodiversity conservation in Australia has found that their non-government status allows them to gain more public support and active participation in their projects by local communities than would be possible if they were a public institution. The Fund has used this to develop community networks to identify and achieve local objectives on covenanted land.

Similarly, local residents in the Garonne Valley in France expressed a low level of trust for both the riparian land owners' ability to sustainably use and conserve the sensitive river bank ecosystem, and the authorities ability to adequately implement, monitor or enforce any necessary measures to encourage such usage. As a result, a survey of residents to determine their willingness to pay for protection measures found almost 50 per cent lodged a protest vote, largely because of a widely-held belief that the public budget is inefficiently allocated.

Even when public authority institutions are responsible for management of the biodiversity resources, non-government organisations or individuals can play a strong role in identifying the concerns and priorities of the affected stakeholders and lobbying the relevant institutions to take the appropriate actions (see Box VI.3 above). They also tend to be responsive to the needs and opinions of the public, and can respond flexibly and quickly to new information and pressures on biodiversity. The New Zealand case study emphasised how the impetus for the purchase and protection of a forested area there came from two public interest groups. This purchase was supported by the Maori tribe who were the private landowners at the time.

In Laganas Bay, Greece, there is a recognised need to increase the involvement of local people in the efforts to preserve the nesting habitats of the loggerhead sea turtle. Since 1987, local authorities have employed 6-9 local wardens for the dissemination of information about the turtles and the safe-guarding of their nests. However, because of local opposition to the project and the temporary, seasonal nature of the employment, this measure had not proven very successful and most of this work is undertaken instead by volunteers, particularly the Sea Turtle Protection Society of Greece.

Similarly, despite early intentions by environmentalists for the development of ecologically-friendly tourism, these plans were not supported by local developers and the tourist operators of big European companies, so rather than successfully entering the market for "green tourism", there has been a development of aggressive, low price, mass tourism in parts of the area, with negative effects on the environment. If an institutional framework had been in place for the better consultation and education of all relevant parties, then it may perhaps have been possible to develop a tourist market that was more compatible with the maintenance of the biodiverse resources on the island.

The implementation of the community forestry project in Turkey has also managed to change the institutional structures of forestry management there for the mutual benefit of all parties concerned. In doing so, it has overcome the traditional conflict between government regulations and restrictions to protect the forest and the need of the villagers to use the forest resources for their survival. Although the implementation of this community forestry project is both time-consuming and costly, it was identified as the most likely incentive to successfully achieve the desired results.

Dedicated resources (including investment) is necessary for the development of suitable institutions and the involvement of stakeholders in the process of designing and implementing appropriate measures for biodiversity conservation and sustainable use. While this may be an expensive process, ensuring that the most suitable measures are applied and that all relevant parties are involved in a co-operative process as far as possible will significantly reduce the costs of monitoring and enforcing the incentive measures in the future.

4. Managing complexity – combinations of incentives to achieve sustainable use

There are a number of reasons why it may be desirable to utilise a combination of incentive measures to tackle the pressures that lead to biodiversity loss. As discussed in Section IV.4 above, a combination of instruments may be needed in order to realise both the public benefits of protecting biodiversity and the private benefits of sustainably using the resources. There are also other reasons why utilising a combination of instruments may be most suitable (Smith, 1998). First, this can provide a "safety valve" effect, whereby if one instrument is insufficient to achieve the desired environmental effect, or is too costly, a second instrument may cut in to alleviate this problem. For example, one can imagine the visitor fee for a nature park being insufficiently high to limit the number of visitors to the optimal level. In

115

Box VII.21. Facts about combinations of instruments

Description: Several instruments, or "hybrid instruments" which aim to achieve more than one single objective.

Advantages: The only way to realise the private *and* the public values of biodiversity.

Disadvantages: Complex instruments which require appropriate capacity and institutions.

Applicability: With few exceptions, most situations in which biodiversity is under pressure.

---

addition to the fee, the park authorities may thus choose to restrict the total number of visitors at particular times through regulations, or employ other measures which limit the effects of the visitors on the ecosystem.

Secondly, they can be particularly useful where the full causal effects of the biodiversity loss are not well understood, as is often the case, or no single instrument exists which can directly target (all of) the causes. As such, a combination of instruments targeting different causes or aspects of the same causal chain will increase the likelihood of the true cause(s) of the loss being "caught" by the policies. Again, where there are particular "hot spots" of biodiversity or its loss, it may be most efficient to design specific instruments to tackle these, while still utilising other instruments to cover the wider ecosystem or target the more general causes of biodiversity loss.

Finally, different categories of biodiversity users will respond differently to particular instruments, so utilising a range of instruments may help to ensure all categories of users are effectively targeted. At the same time, there may be distributional or competitiveness reasons in some situations such that authorities may wish to allow certain user groups (for example, indigenous peoples) greater or less access to the resources than others. In such cases, it may be desirable to use combinations of instruments which are targeted to the different user groups.

Most of the case studies undertaken for this project emphasised the importance of utilising a mix of incentive measures. The studies from Japan, Korea and Greece in particular emphasised the benefits of combining a mix of regulatory restrictions with more market-based and educational/stakeholder-involvement approaches. The Oze National Park in Japan provides a particularly interesting example of the use of a mix of instruments for the successful protection of biodiversity, including the clear definition of property rights, the establishment of an environmental fund, the restriction and regulation of particular harmful activities, the provision of physical infrastructure to protect the natural habitat from human impacts, and the use of a strong environmental educational and awareness-raising programme both in the Park itself and nationally.

In Korea, authorities focused conservation activities around the protection of an extremely endangered keystone species, the Asiatic black bear. Here, the responsibility of the different aspects relating to the protection of the bear was moved under one co-ordinated body, killing of the bears was prohibited (with the prohibition being strongly enforced), efforts were made to enhance the value of protecting the bear for local communities, active participation by NGOs in the protection of the species was encouraged, subsidies which promoted the destruction of its natural habitat were removed, and physical infrastructure was provided for its protection and ease of movement. In Greece, a similar mix of regulations, park creation, educational activities, stakeholder involvement and physical infrastructure provision has been used to protect the nesting areas of the endangered loggerhead turtle.

As in Korea and Greece, both the Mexican and the Turkish case studies emphasised the development of incentive measures which provided economic incentives for local communities to sustainably use or conserve the biological resources in combination with strong educational programmes and regulatory measures. Even where national parks of biosphere reserves are created to provide for the strict protection of vulnerable ecosystems, additional incentive measures may be used to ensure the co-operation of stakeholders, as was the case in Austria where hunters were compensated for the restrictions on their hunting activities.

Other studies emphasised the use of combinations of non-regulatory instruments. For example, in the UK, a combination of environmental fund, educational activities, scientific research and the reform of adverse subsidies to tie them to environmental improvements have been used to protect the heathlands. In Finland as well, the development of a forest certification scheme was accompanied by the removal of adverse subsidies for the unsustainable use of forestry resources.

Effective policy action will thus combine several incentive measures in carefully calibrated packages addressing the multiple objectives of, and the impediments to, the conservation and the sustainable use of biodiversity. The most promising approach is the encouragement of private activities under certain conditions which ensure their contribution to the conservation of biodiversity. Young and Gunningham (1997) go so far as to recommend that:

> ... emphasis on dependability and precaution means that the most cost-effective instrument mix will include mechanisms and instruments that appear to be redundant but are there because from time to time other instruments or institutions are expected to fail.

Of course, such redundancy, while desirable in biodiversity terms, also has its costs in terms of establishing and managing competing layers of administrations and a number of potential problems. First, using more than one policy instrument can be wasteful where the instruments are too closely directed to the same objective and overlap. In some cases, usually only one of the instruments – the stricter one – will actually "bite", while the other(s) may be ineffective. As indicated above, however, some overlap between policies can be useful where the policies are directed at areas with substantial uncertainty or threshold effects, as are often found in biodiversity. However, such overlap should be deliberately designed to target those areas where it may be most beneficial, in order to ensure administrative and compliance costs are kept to a minimum.

Secondly, the instrument mix needs to be carefully designed to avoid any potential conflicts between the individual instruments, and to ensure that all activities that should be addressed actually are. Some of these difficulties can be avoided through careful design of the instrument mix. There exist no silver bullets; it only with diligence and patience that the effective policy mix can be developed. In order to ensure transparency and comprehensibility of biodiversity policies, it is best that the incentive measures used are kept as simple as possible and directly targeted to the underlying causes of biodiversity loss.

Annex 1

Framework for Case Studies

The basis for the practical experience of the design and implementation of incentive measures developed in this *Handbook* was drawn from the twenty-two case studies provided by OECD Member countries. All the case studies were prepared according to the structure outlined in the "Incentive Measures to Promote the Conservation and Sustainable Use of Biodiversity: Framework for Case Studies" (OECD, 1997*a*) developed by the OECD Expert Group on the Economic Aspects of Biodiversity. The basic structure of the framework is described briefly below. The full text (document number OCDE/GD(97)125) can be accessed at the OECD Internet site at http://www.oecd.org/env.

Because the case studies utilised this common Framework for analysis, it is possible to compare the results they derive from the application of different incentive measures in terms of the sources of the initial pressures on biodiversity, the environmental, economic and social effects of these pressures, and the design, implementation and effects of the incentive measures used. The use of this Framework can assist policy-makers to identify case studies with similar elements to their own biodiversity problems, and from which they can draw policy-relevant advice for the design and application of their own incentive measures. Not only was the Framework used for the OECD case studies, but it has also been adopted by the Secretariat of the Convention on Biological Diversity as the basis for its case study work.

In addition to evolving into a standard for the analysis of case studies, the Framework can also be used as a structure for the design of new case studies. The more comparable the various case studies on biodiversity incentive measures are, the more useful they will be to policy makers and analysts. Comparability of the case studies is essential to be able to draw generalisable policy conclusions.

In the following, the framework is presented in detail, chapter by chapter, including comments that highlight the sort of information most useful in the preparation of the case studies. It is estimated that the total length of a typical case study may vary between 18 and 25 pages. For each section described below, estimated chapter lengths are provided as a rough guide for *relative* weights.

Chapter 1. **General description**
  - Description of the ecosystem
  - Description of main impacts

- Identification of incentive measure
- Identification of economic sector(s) targeted by incentive measure

Chapter 1 sets the stage for the case study and should enable the reader to relate the more detailed information provided in later chapters. It should also identify those elements of biodiversity that are the primary objective of the policy action, such as particular indicators or species. Chapter 1 should contain on one page an indication of the most important issues the case study will focus on.

Chapter 2.   Identification of causes and sources of pressures

Chapter 2 identifies in progressive steps the reasons for the biodiversity loss or the threats thereof. It proceeds from a description of the most manifest causes of biodiversity loss to a description of underlying policy failures in keeping with the framework developed in *Saving Biological Diversity: Economic Incentives* (OECD, 1996). An additional step will analyse adverse incentives that promote activities that cause pressure on biodiversity.

Section 2.1.   Identification of sectoral activities and resulting pressures through

- Pollution
- Conversion and land-use
- Non-sustainable use of biological diversity, including species trade

The lack of adequate incentives and hence the missing reflection of the value of biological diversity in policy making translates itself through several "channels". Their identification is the purpose of Section 2.1. These channels are examples for unsustainable patterns of consumption and production as described in Section 3.2 of *Saving Biological Diversity*. Pollution through industrial, agricultural or touristic activities is an important and well-studied channel of the underlying causes that lead to pressures on biological diversity, especially in areas of intense economic activity. To the extent that sectoral activities and consumption patterns have beneficial effects on biological diversity, such as in certain forms of mountain agriculture, these should also be mentioned.

The most important channel in areas without traditional economic activity, however, is land conversion. This takes the form that land is converted from a use (or non-use) that allows abundant biological diversity but yields no or low private economic benefits to uses that allow only low biological diversity but yield higher economic benefits. Examples are the conversion of natural grasslands or natural forests into land for agriculture, human settlements or industrial forestry. To the extent that land use and conversion are linked to problems of population growth and migration this should also be highlighted.

A third category of transmission channels is constituted by the unsustainable use of biological diversity. Unsustainable use implies that biodiversity resources are used suboptimally. This sub-optimality refers to three distinct instances:

- short-term exploitation takes precedence over the maximisation of long-term benefits;
- the exploitation of the target resource (*e.g.*, a certain tropical wood) destroys the surrounding ecosystem; or

– the value of the resource is, even in the short-run, insufficiently realised as exploitation proceeds on a first-come, first-serve basis and not on a willingness-to-pay basis which would give rights to the highest value use.

Well-known examples in this category are the over-exploitation of fish stocks, the harvesting of tropical timber and the trade in rare, exotic species. The economic analysis of these processes is analogous to the analysis of rapid rent-dissipation in unmanaged open access regimes ("tragedy of the commons").[37]

Section 2.1 can be relatively short, about one to two pages. While it would be desirable to link it to the underlying conceptual considerations, theses considerations have not, in themselves to be repeated in connection with the single case studies.

Section 2.2. Identification of underlying causes of biodiversity loss

- Missing markets or non-existent property rights
- Information failure
- Institutional failure
- Enforcement failure
- Failure to adequately consider the lifestyles of indigenous and local communities

The driving forces of biodiversity loss can be approached on different levels and can be grouped according to different categories. *Saving Biological Diversity* had chosen in the chapter on "Underlying causes" the three subheadings

– consumption and production patterns;
– patterns of population growth and distribution; and
– economic failures.

Global increases in per capita consumption of energy and natural resources in combination with unsustainable systems of agricultural and industrial production, are driving habitat conversion and degradation world-wide. Unsustainable patterns of consumption and production must be addressed through a broad range of policy mechanisms. Population growth and population distribution lead to pressure on land and aquatic resources, especially for food production but also for infrastructure such as roads and housing. Even regional population distribution, such as increased urbanisation and high concentration densities along coastlines and other waterways, can result in destruction of, or damage to terrestrial, aquatic, and marine biodiversity.

These underlying causes of biodiversity loss can be understood in the context of the failures of economic mechanisms. This section examines categories relating to lack of information and institutions that contribute to, or fail to correct for, these underlying causes of biodiversity loss. This allows the consideration of the issues in a perspective that can lead directly to positive policy action correcting those failures and to alleviate the pressures on biological diversity.

Proceeding from the identification of the channels through which the lack of appropriate incentives translates itself into the loss of or a threat to biological diversity, Section 2.2 presents the underlying causes itself. The loss of biological diversity is the result of the lack of appropriate mechanisms to reflect its value. This can relate to the non-realisation of the private use value of biological diversity or of its public good value. Since biological diversity usually embodies private as well as public values, policy failure can, and frequently does, relate to both aspects. Section 2.3, however, should as far as possible concentrate on the *underlying failure of economic mechanisms* to adequately reflect the value of biodiversity in private actions.

The private value of biological diversity is equal to the sum of all of its privately appropriable benefits suitably discounted over the long-run. It includes, for instance, the use of biodiversity for eco-tourism, as a pool for genetic resources, or for the sustainable exploitation of certain plants, products or animals. The allocation of secure and enforceable property rights is in this case the single most important step. However, in realising the full private value of biological diversity through the allocation of property rights that allows markets to arise two points have to be considered.

First, are the property rights going to the party whose use would yield the highest potential value? Of course, property rights are, in principle, tradable. However, in a complex area such as biological diversity significant transactions costs exist and the initial assignment of property rights might determine the use to a very large degree. Second, lack of information might induce users, as well as policy makers, to pursue, or promote, comparatively low value uses over high value uses.

Biological diversity in all its variety also contains significant option value for private as well as public use. While a private owner with perfect foresight would realise the full private option value, an insufficiently informed owner would not. Considering the current, insufficient, state of knowledge about the processes involved in biological diversity, an argument for ensuring a certain margin of safety, in accordance with the precautionary principle, should be made.

At least in some cases, even the realisation of the full private value of biological diversity will not be sufficient to compete with alternative land-uses such as industrial uses, the planting of agricultural monocrops, or the building of human settlements. Yet nevertheless, there might exist a policy consensus that the conservation and the sustainable use of the ecosystem in question is warranted for reasons of the maintenance of national heritage, as a reservoir for clean air and water or the deriving of pleasure from the pure knowledge of its existence. In those cases, policy will have to realise the *public good value* of biological diversity that can include its private value.

The simplest measure is, of course, to fence off the area and to forbid access. However, subtler measures, and possibly more cost-effective ones, are feasible, in particular, in combination with the realisation of private value. Sustainable private uses can contribute to the maintenance of ecosystems and can thus also realise and even enhance their public goods value. However, such sustainable uses can be privately less profitable than unsustainable uses. In those cases, covering the short-fall through public expenditures can be a possible solution.[38] An added benefit to such a solution could also be cost savings due to a reduction of monitoring and enforcement costs (see Section 5.2).

The task of Section 2.2 is to identify as precisely as possible the extent to which the policy failure relates to the non-realisation of the private or the public good value of the ecosystem studied. Section 5.1 will discuss the chosen incentive measure chosen to address the policy failure directly. However, the analysis in Section 2.2 of the character of the policy failure should be the starting point for the choice of the incentive measure designed to remediate the policy failure. Indicatively, Section 2.2 should be of two pages of length.

Section 2.3. *Identification of adverse incentives, including*

- Direct and indirect subsidies
- Market price supports
- Tax incentives
- Infrastructure provision

While Section 2.2 should identify the *lack* of appropriate policies to conserve or sustainably use biological diversity, Section 2.3 should identify those policies that actively *promote* activities that are detrimental to biological diversity. Frequently, both kinds of policy failure exist together, as both are the result of an inadequate reflection of the value of biological diversity in policy making. As a policy action (see Section 5.1) adverse incentives do not require an introduction of additional policies but the removal or reform of existing policies.

Adverse incentives are incentives that promote behaviour that reduces biodiversity. They include direct and indirect subsidies, whether as direct transfers, import protection or beneficial tax treatment ("tax incentives"). They also include the provision of infrastructure out of general tax receipts that over-proportionally benefit a particular sector with adverse impacts, such as roads that provide access to sensitive ecosystems that would otherwise be more costly to accede.

The analysis of incentives to activities adverse to biological diversity lends itself to a sectoral approach. Adverse incentives are usually provided due to policy objectives other than the conservation or the sustainable use of biological diversity. These objectives are connected to specific sectors, *e.g.*, energy, agriculture, transport, fisheries, of whose activities positive spill-overs such as social cohesion, regional development or an improvement of the trade balance are expected.

The adverse incentives can pertain to a macro-level, such as in the case of tax breaks or import protection for an entire industry, or to a micro-level, such as in the case of a specific extension of infrastructure. It is important to identify the original policy objectives connected with the provision of adverse incentives and the resulting distributional consequences (see also Section 5.2 on "Process of implementation and distributional effects"). Since Section 2.3 is concerned with the identification rather than the discussion of the effects of adverse incentives its length should not exceed one to two pages.

Chapter 3. Impacts on ecosystems

- Impacts on genetic and species diversity
- Impacts on ecosystem in general
- Impact on most important (*e.g.*, keystone, indicator, economic or cultural) species
- Impacts on ecosystem resilience
- Damage to resource base

Chapter 3 should provide the most pertinent scientific information about the biological, chemical and physical situation in which the case study takes place. In keeping with the approach outlined in *Saving Biological Diversity* an ecosystem approach is recommended. Detailed information on genetic and species diversity is, of course, welcome, but should be related to the wider habitat, community or ecosystem. It is important that those aspects that posed the original cause for policy concern are highlighted. Of particular importance are in this context the concepts of "keystone species" and "ecosystem resilience".

The two related concepts refer to the long-run sustainability of a habitat or ecosystem as a definable ensemble of biological functions. Keystone species are particular species in a particular habitat or ecosystem that assume a critical role for its resistance to adverse pressures, *i.e.* its resilience. The identification of a particular species, either as an indicator or as a crucial ecological link, allows policy efforts towards conservation and sustainable use to concentrate on single elements of the ecosystem in the choice of incentive measures as well as in the definition of indicators for monitoring and enforcement.

Frequently, also public opinion crystallises around keystone or indicator species, as they become widely recognised symbols of the ecosystems to which they belong. Thus concern about the survival of a particular species is substituted for a less easily communicable concern for the state of an ecosystem. A good example for this process are the discussions in the Pacific Northwest of the United States, where the survival of the spotted owl is dependent on the preservation and the sustainable management of old-growth forests.

The health and sustainability of keystone species can also be one indicator for the resilience of a habitat or ecosystem. The preservation of an ecosystem in a pristine state, free from all human interaction, can be the objective only of a limited number of conservation efforts. In all other instances, the ability of an ecosystem to react and to a certain extent adapt to human interaction is crucial. The importance of the resilience of an ecosystem lies in this ability to adapt while maintaining its distinctive features.

In particular, resilience refers to the ability to maintain the integrity of ecological functions. These ecological functions include those that are *directly* valued by humans, for instance, aesthetic beauty, but also those that are *indirectly* valued through the "services" they render to economic sectors, such as agriculture, forestry, fisheries or tourism by absorbing pollution, providing and maintaining commercially valuable species or by serving as genetic reservoir. Ecosystem resilience is thus closely related, but not identical to the maintenance of the species contained in it. At least over a limited time-period, the variety of species could, in principle, be maintained, while ecological functions and resilience are already damaged.

Since Chapter 3 is providing a host of biological, chemical and physical information, its length should, indicatively, be three to five pages.

Chapter 4.   Impacts on economy and welfare
- Direct economic losses
- Economic valuation of damages to public goods (if applicable)
- Effects of adverse incentives on budget, efficiency and employment
- Beneficiaries of inaction and bearers of costs prior to implementation

Activities that cause damages to biological diversity and ecosystems have direct and indirect impacts on human welfare. These impacts can be differentiated in three categories –

direct economic impacts, damages to public goods connected with biodiversity and economic impacts of adverse incentives. First, there are those impacts that directly affect economic activities. This can include the valuation of "traditional" economically valuable resources such as, for instance, minerals, timber or fresh water. It also includes reductions to the value of activities that sustainably use biodiversity, such as eco-tourism. These damages translate into private losses for individuals working in the sectors concerned. This first category of economic impacts also includes damages to potential benefits from the utilisation of genetic resources.

Second, there are impacts on public goods connected with biodiversity, such as existence and option values for distinct species or ecosystems, *i.e.*, the appreciation for their beauty and their being part of nature. While a series of methods for the monetary evaluation of these public good values are available, the ecosystem approach to biological diversity suggests caution in the interpretation of the derived values: the monetary expression of the value of single elements of biological diversity necessarily implies the isolated consideration of these elements. One value of biological diversity lies in the interconnection of a multitude of biological elements and functions and in the complexity this generates. Thus in the case of biological diversity, the monetary expression of any of its elements will only capture a fraction of its value as part of a larger ensemble.

Economic valuation can be highly valuable for the focusing of public opinion as well as for the guidance of policy by helping to integrate biodiversity concerns into economic decision-making. It can be an incentive measure on its own by correcting for information failures or it can provide valuable input for the development of incentive measures. However, while helpful in certain policy contexts, the monetary valuation of damages to biodiversity is not required for the implementation of incentive measures.

Third, the economic pressures and adverse incentives discussed in Section 2.3 can have adverse impacts not only on biological diversity. The abolition of subsidies, for instance would reduce the burden on government budgets and, *a priori*, increase economic efficiency. Thus, in principle, their removal can bring beneficial economic as well as ecological benefits. Of course, the cost of subsidy removal comes in terms of those alternative policy objectives that were originally pursued with the help of subsidies.

The individual case studies on the implementation of incentive measures for the conservation and the sustainable use of biological diversity are not the place to engage in an extended analysis of the general arguments against the provision of government support for single industries. It is necessary though that *all* impacts of government actions, including adverse impacts on biodiversity, costs to tax payers, economic efficiencies and employment considerations receive adequate attention.

The costs to government budgets of the support to sectors or activities with negative impacts on biodiversity should be clearly stated. The employment results *with* the adverse incentive in place should also be briefly contrasted with the employment effects of a sustainable use of the biodiversity resource in question, in the absence of adverse incentives. Employment created by the sustainable use of biodiversity has the added advantage of being able to provide employment for indigenous populations, whose knowledge and practices could thereby be profitably maintained.

125|

In addition to those three categories of economic damages, those groups that carry the main burden of these costs, as well as those groups that benefit from the situation *without* incentive measures to conserve and sustainably biodiversity should be clearly identified. Chapter 4 should comprise about two to three pages.

Chapter 5.   Implementation of incentive measure(s) and context

Chapter 5 is concerned with the incentive measure chosen in each case study and its implementation process. Chapter 3 has analysed the situation that requires the implementation of incentive measures. Chapter 4 has brought together any related information on economic impacts. Chapter 5 draws together the information about the actual measure designed to remediate that situation. Particular emphasis is paid in this context to issues of stakeholder involvement, distribution, institutional development, the social and cultural context and the generation and dissemination of information.

Section 5.1.   *Identification of actual or planned incentive measure*

- Category of measure (regulation, market incentive, property rights definition etc.)
- Objective of incentive measure
- Reason for choosing measure

Incentive measures for the conservation and the sustainable use of biological diversity are means to induce individual agents to include the full private and public value of biological diversity in their economic decisions. Section 5.1 should identify and describe the proposed or implemented incentive measure of each case study. Of particular interest are those incentives that rely on private behaviour in markets for a transmission of this value. As a basis for identification could be employed the table on page nine of *Saving Biological Diversity: Economic Incentives*. The table distinguishes between positive incentives, disincentives, indirect incentives and the removal of perverse incentives.

A different set of categories could be constituted by: first, measures that realise the private use value of biodiversity through the creation of property rights and markets; second, measures that realise the value of biological diversity as a public good through instruments such as environmental taxes, standards, a transferable quota systems or the creation of a protected area; and third, the reduction of uncertainty and an increase in information in order to avoid unsustainable short-term exploitation of resources. The measures should correspond to the analysis of the policy failure in Section 2.2 that was at the bottom of the pressure on biological diversity.

Related to these points Section 5.1 should also briefly discuss the precise objective of the measure as part of the overall aim to conserve and sustainably use biodiversity, as well as the actual reason it was ultimately selected for. In a real world context, the two might differ. In discussing the reasons for choosing the measure also any methods of analysis, in particular economic analysis, that might have been employed by the policy-implementing decision-maker should be referred to. This might include cost-benefit analysis, including the economic value of biodiversity, input-output analysis, scenario analysis or others.

Section 5.1 should, nevertheless, not be longer than one to two pages, since much of the background has already been prepared in Sections 2.1-2.3.

Section 5.2. *Process of implementation and distributional effects*

- Beneficiaries of incentive measure and bearers of cost after implementation
- Participation and negotiation
- Enforcement and compliance

Section 5.2 would contain a short description of the actual *process* of implementation. It would draw together the single elements and describe how they lead up to the implementation of the incentive measure over time. In this subchapter particular attention should be paid to the time dimension. The implementation of an incentive measure ranges from the first identification of adverse pressures on biological diversity over the analysis of underlying causes, over the build up of policy support for remedial action, over the selection of an appropriate incentive measure and over its legal implementation to, in last instance, its enforcement. Section 5.2 should trace this evolution.

Incentive measures that support the conservation and sustainable use of biological diversity by realising its true private and public value contribute to the maximisation of total societal welfare. However, this does not mean that *everybody* profits from the implementation of an incentive measure. It just implies that the benefits from an appropriately chosen and implemented incentive measure outweigh its costs. In principle, this would imply that the winners from the implementation of an incentive measure could compensate the losers, whose welfare would stay constant, while increasing their own (and total) welfare.

Ideally, such compensation would take place and there would be *only* winners from the implementation of an incentive measure. In practice however, such compensation does not always take place. There will thus be winners and losers from the implementation of an incentive measure, as there were winners and losers from the absence of incentive measures. Thus even when the implementation of an incentive measure remedies an inefficient situation, and hence increases total welfare, there are potentially groups that will lose, since they profited in the past from unsustainable use (see Chapter 4.).

This has impacts on the feasibility of the incentive measure. To the extent that biological diversity is a public good the number of people that benefit from its protection will be a large, while the benefit itself will be relatively small for each person. On the contrary, the beneficiaries from unsustainable short-term use in the absence of appropriate incentive measures might be few in number but their individual benefits might be relatively high. Although total benefits from protection will outweigh the costs due to the high number of beneficiaries, it is frequently taken for a fact that the interests of small, well-organised interest groups with individually large stakes will have an easier time to be heard and to influence policy than the interests of large groups with individually small stakes. Similar effects can arise in conflicts between long-term and short-term interests.

The maximisation of total welfare through the appropriate consideration of biodiversity concerns indicates *a priori* little about the fact whether the distributional impacts of incentive measures for the conservation and the sustainable use of biological diversity are desirable or not. However, incentive measures that promote the wider application of practices relevant for the sustainable use of biodiversity through indigenous and local communities, and that

127

would presumably make the latter "the winners" of such an incentive measure, do receive additional support from Article 8(j) of the Convention on Biological Diversity. Of course, all distributional issues take place in the context of Article 3 of the Convention that states the sovereign right of states over their resources.

The solution of distributional questions directly relates to questions of stakeholder participation in the implementation process and any negotiations that have preceded or accompanied it. Relevant questions in this context are: have groups concerned either by the environmental impacts or the implementation of the incentive measure been consulted in advance? Did these groups have a possibility to voice their concerns during the process? And finally, how does the process of implementation relate to other regional, national, or international initiatives.

Particular emphasis should, finally, be on those aspects that become relevant *after* the legal enactment and institutionalisation of an incentive measure. Thus questions of compliance and, if applicable, enforcement should be discussed. Compliance and enforcement are closely linked to the question of the distributional impacts of the incentive measure and how they further or hinder the process of implementation. Compensation schemes for losers, for instance, might increase the feasibility of incentive measures by reducing monitoring and the enforcement costs. A complete analysis of the costs of the measure will thus have to firmly link efficiency and distributional considerations. The length of Section 5.2 could vary between two and three pages.

Section 5.3. *The role of information and uncertainty in the implementation process*

- Information about biodiversity value and environmental impacts
- Information about economic impacts
- Technical information
- Cultural (indigenous) knowledge

Information, its generation and distribution, or the lack of it, permeates every aspect of biodiversity policies. The lack of information about the value of biodiversity does not allow its adequate conservation, or fails to make its use sustainable. Lack of information is equivalent to uncertainty about the trade-offs between the benefits of biological diversity and the economic activities that diminish these benefits. The role of information is also directly linked to the cultural and social context. Attitudes and perceptions are shaped by different sets of information. The provision and dissemination of information about the different private and public values of biological diversity have a direct impact on the cultural patterns and are part of the successful implementation of incentive measures.

The provision of information about the value of biological diversity can in itself constitute an incentive measure. To the extent that the loss of biological diversity is perceived as a loss of welfare comparable to the costs and benefits of economic activities, the value of biodiversity can be integrated through market-based instruments into economic decision making. However, care has to be taken in the choice of incentive measures as information can be asymmetric. In such cases, the distributional impact of the incentive measure can have additional (and frequently unforeseen) incentive effects on the provision and availability of information in the first place (see Section 5.2).

A good example of asymmetric information and the impact it has on the choice of incentive mechanisms is constituted by the "first mover problem": if a landowner finds a commercially useless species that is threatened by extinction on his property, his economically rational action would be to hide its existence, if the incentive mechanism to conserve biodiversity is constituted by a regulation that restricts commercially attractive activities. His action might be different, if the incentive mechanism is constituted by a different regulation that imposes restrictions only in combination with, for instance, a property tax rebate for land with a high biodiversity value, reflecting the public interest. It would be helpful, if case study authors could identify similar problems in the course of the experience described and outline any means that have been chosen to deal with them.

Another particular aspect of information in the sphere of biological diversity consists in the importance of the "knowledge, innovations, and practices of indigenous and local communities embodying traditional lifestyles relevant for the conservation and the sustainable use of biodiversity" and the protection accorded to them under the Convention on Biological Diversity. Such traditional knowledge can also offer useful guidance towards methods of resource management and conservation (*e.g.*, frequency of prescribed fires for weed control). To some extent this special kind of information is part of biodiversity itself and thus becomes an objective, as well as an instrument, of conservation and sustainable use.

Last not least, the question how the available scientific information relating to physical, chemical and biological facts has been treated in the design, implementation and the evaluation of an incentive measure is an important element of the case study. Indicators such as "number of species", for instance, can constitute a basis for determining a need for action or in establishing the success or failure of an incentive measure. In this context not the information itself (which should have been contained in Chapter 2) is relevant, but its strategic use in implementing the incentive measures.

Section 5.3 should thus also refer to the state of (scientific) knowledge on the basis of which the decision to implement an economic incentive measure has been made. It should also, if applicable, indicate research efforts that accompanied the implementation of the incentive measure. Its total length should be around two pages.

Section 5.4. *Framework and context of implementation*

- Explicit legal framework, property and use rights (formal constraints)
- Cultural, historical and social context (social constraints)
- Institutions concerned (including appropriate government level)
- Internal evaluation and remedial process

As highlighted in Section 2.2 unsustainable pressures on biological result from policy failures. These policy omissions, while leading to suboptimal situations, are part of an established legal and institutional framework. The introduction of incentive measures is thus about legal and institutional change. In some cases, the institutional framework is well laid out to accommodate new and changed circumstances, in other cases this might not be the case. Implementation will then require additional transaction costs in terms of changing institutions or setting up new ones. The task of Section 5.4 is to highlight the different legal, institutional and cultural processes that are taking place in the implementation on an incentive measure.

The formal institutional and legal framework conditions should be treated briefly, but precisely. The main decision makers in the implementation of the incentive measure, and, if applicable, the processes involved in any appeal against this implementation should be indicated. Also those institutions or actors concerned with monitoring and enforcement should be briefly introduced. Of course, any new institutions created in the process of implementation need also to be mentioned.

Of great importance for the successful implementation of incentive measures are so-called social constraints, or the cultural, historical and social context. They are particularly relevant since the conservation and the sustainable use of biological diversity involves the transfer of a frequently only vaguely perceived "public" good from an informal domain of costless access and use into a more structured sphere where single elements of biological diversity are "valorised" in different dimensions such as genetic resource value, recreational value, option and existence values and so forth. If this transfer is to be successful, long-standing perceptions and behavioural patters of the relevant actors have either to be positively reinforced by the incentive measure or to change, sometimes radically so.

The success of the implementation of an incentive measure will frequently depend on the degree to which the implementation process manages to integrate the social and cultural context. It is important that the incentive measure implemented works in a fashion that is complementary rather than contradictory to the existing cultural context. It should work within this context, wherever compatible with the conservation and the sustainable use of biodiversity. The basis for such compatibility is the diligent study of the context, mutual consultation and information, and, in last instance, adaptation of the incentive measure.

Finally, the question should be answered, whether an internal evaluation (as opposed to an external evaluation such as the present OECD effort) of the success of the incentive measure exists. Last not least, it would be of interest if the implementation process foresees any mechanism to re-adjust the incentive measure after first experiences. Preliminary evidence suggests that only measures designed for at least a medium time horizon would have any beneficial impacts on the conservation and the sustainable use of biological diversity. This would make the existence (or non-existence) of such review mechanisms an interesting point to discuss. Due to its importance, Section 5.4 can be of up to three pages of length.

Chapter 6.   Policy relevant conclusions

Chapter 6 will contain those elements most relevant for policy guidance on the implementation of incentive measures. In fact, it should provide, from the perspective of individual authors, a short interpretation of the results of the preceding three chapters with respect to their relevance for general policy conclusions.

Section 6.1.   Lessons learned

Section 6.1 should contain a first synthesis of the case study with regard to the projected or actual effectiveness of the incentive measure implemented and the determinants of its success, or failure. Despite its importance, this synthesis can be short and highlight on one page only the most important lessons learned.

Section 6.2. *Transferability of the experience*

As a second step, a short comment should be provided on the extent to which the case study could be considered representative. The particularities of the case study should be evaluated whether they constitute fundamental barriers to the transferability of the results to other instances. Of course, each case will have its unique characteristics. However in some cases, these characteristics may not regard the fundamental working of the incentive measures. In other cases, the particularities will be such that the incentive measure under consideration will not display the same characteristics in other situations.

Minimum requirements concerning the transferability of the experience, such as minimum institutional requirements, minimum biotic or ecological requirements and market requirements should also be mentioned. The length of this discussion should not exceed one page.

Section 6.3. *Possible policy advice for implementation*

Section 6.3 should contain a first indication by the authors of the individual case studies which general policy conclusions could be drawn from their case study. In addition, the single greatest barrier and the single greatest positive influence towards success of the implementation of the incentive measure should be identified. Again, these elements for possible policy conclusion should be delivered on one page or less.

OECD 1999

Annex 2
Overview of Case Studies

A brief summary of each of the case studies produced by Member countries for this report is presented below, accompanied by the ecosystem(s) studied, the incentive measures used, the main lessons learned and the relevant contact details for further information. The full reports of each study is available on the OECD Internet site at http://www.oecd.org/env/eco/.

Australia
A Revolving Fund for Biodiversity Conservation in Australia
Author: Marc Carter

Summary: This case study examines the role played by the Revolving Fund for Nature, administered by the Trust for Nature (Victoria), in the protection of lands of conservation significance, particularly those with remnant or heritage vegetation. The Revolving Fund purchases lands with conservation significance, places a covenant on them specifying the allowable and prohibited activities that can be undertaken on them, thus ensuring the future maintenance of the identified conservation values, and resells the lands to a sympathetic private owner whose use of the lands will be bound by the covenant. The regained capital is then used to finance the purchase of further lands, which again have a covenant placed on them before resale to sympathetic purchasers and the process is repeated again. The success of the Fund relies largely on its ability to recapture all or most of the original capital purchase cost for the lands, and to pass on responsibility for land management to owners who are committed to a conservation ethic. The fund is unique in that the Trust for Nature was formed through government legislation and is provided with some public funding but also attracts funds from non-government sources.

Ecosystems studied: arable lands, grasslands, forests.

Incentive measures used: environmental fund, permits, covenants, removal of adverse tax incentives.

Main lessons learned: A balance needs to be set between the amount of funds directed towards purchasing properties at any point in time and the amount kept in reserve funds; human habitation must be possible on the sites for purchase; it was found that the Fund has positive indirect effects in terms of promoting conservation ideals and facilitating land exchanges by government conservation agencies.

Contact details of delegate:

Ms Veronika BLAZELY
Environment Australia
Biodiversity Group
GPO Box 787
CANBERRA, ACT 2601

Fax: (61 6) 250 0723
email: Veronica.Blazely@ea.gov.au

Austria
Economic Incentive Measures in the Creation
of the National Park Neusiedler See – Seewinkel
Authors: Klaus Hubacek and Wolfgang Bauer

Summary: This case study examines the use of economic incentives for the establishment and running of the National Park Neusiedler See (Seewinkel). The Park was opened in 1983 and was the first National Park in Austria recognised under Category II by the IUCN. A number of incentive measures were used to ensure the conservation of the Neusiedler See and the reedbelt there (recognised as a biosphere reserve by UNESCO in 1977). These include the removal of government subsidies for the drainage of the wetlands for agricultural cultivation, the provision of compensation to land owners ceding their lands to the National Park, restricting the access of hunters to the area (with compensation for entitled hunters), the possible ceasing of the stocking of the lake with non-native fish species (again with potential compensation), and the banning of reed burning while allowing the continued, sustainable, harvesting of the reeds. Because of falling prices and growing intensification in agriculture, as well as increased tourism activities, the National Park is seen as a positive economic alternative to agriculture.

Ecosystem studied: inland freshwater ecosystems.

Incentive measures used: access restrictions (national park creation), removal of adverse incentives, compensation for use restrictions.

Main lessons learned: The use of a combination of economic incentives, information dissemination, and paying individuals compensation for restricting their use of the lands was particularly successful; compensation was found to be necessary in particular where the pressures on biodiversity came from outside the Park boundaries.

Contact details of delegate:

Mr. Manfred SCHNEIDER
Bundesministerium für Umwelt, Jugend und Familie
Präs. 5, Internationale Angelegenheiten und EU   Tel.: (43 1) 515 22 1608
Stubenbastei 5   Fax: (43 1) 515 22 7624
A-1010 VIENNA   Email: Manfred.Schneider_M@bmu.gv.at

OECD 1999

Austria
The Austrian Programme on Environmentally Sound and Sustainable Agriculture: Experiences and Consequences of Sustainable Use of Biodiversity in Austrian Agriculture
Authors: Josef Hoppichler and Michael Groier

Summary: This case study examines a programme for encouraging the environmentally sound and sustainable management of agriculture in Austria, primarily through the use of agri-environmental subsidies under the EU Regulation 2078/92. The Austrian agricultural subsidy programmes were restructured and re-oriented in the late 1980s and early 1990s, with particular emphasis placed on agri-ecological aspects of funding and the integration of environment-related direct payments into the funding system. The incentives used include soil protection charges and taxes, the Law on Water Rights (*e.g.* binding livestock to the region), regulations specifying maximum limits for livestock numbers, and the funding of organic farming, crop rotation, and land set-aside schemes. In order to ensure the benefits from these measures were maintained once Austria joined the EU, an integral horizontal approach for the Austrian agri-environmental programme was developed under EU Regulation 2078/92. The programme utilises a range of subsidies to encourage less environmentally-harmful agricultural practices, while taking into consideration socio-economic factors as well.

Ecosystem studied: arable lands.

Incentive measures used: positive subsidies, market creation, removal of adverse incentives, information provision.

Main lessons learned: European, national, and regional considerations have to be reconciled; political consensus is of great importance for successful implementation; and appropriate public relations work is necessary.

Contact details of delegate:

Mr. Manfred SCHNEIDER
Bundesministerium für Umwelt, Jugend und Familie
Präs. 5, Internationale Angelegenheiten und EU
Stubenbastei 5
A-1010 VIENNA

Tel.: (43 1) 515 22 1608
Fax: (43 1) 515 22 7624
Email: Manfred.Schneider_M@bmu.gv.at

Canada
Revealing the Economic Value of Biodiversity:
A New Incentive Measure to Conserve and Protect It
Authors: Fern Filion, Jim Frehs and Darryl Sprecher

Summary: This case study revisits the benefit cost analysis of a project to develop a reservoir on the Canadian prairies to provide water for agricultural production, tourism and municipal needs in order to add to the original monetised private goods estimates the public goods benefits and costs of the effects on biodiversity. The Environmental Valuation Reference Inventory was used to find valuation studies conducted in similar situations from which estimates of the values of the effects in this project could be drawn (benefits transfer). In the original study, both the economic costs and benefits of the project were valued to be CAN$ 76.5 million. The original study also identified some non-quantifiable environmental benefits and costs from the project, which an assessment panel concluded would tend to result in an overall net benefit, thus improving the relative economic effects of the project. As a result, the reservoir was constructed. Once the benefits transfer exercise was conducted – and drawing on studies that utilised contingent valuation and travel cost methods for determining the environmental values – it was found that the revised BCA for the project would result in a net loss of approximately CAN$ 10 million.

Ecosystems studied: grasslands, rangelands, inland freshwater ecosystems, forests.

Incentive measures used: economic valuation, information provision.

Main lessons learned: Public economic values of biodiversity can be revealed through economic valuation using a benefits-transfer approach, thus mitigating information failures; this is a very cost-effective means of producing monetary values for biodiversity goods and services.

Contact details of delegate:

Mr. Fernand L. FILION
Director, Environmental Economics Branch
Environment Canada
7th Floor, Place Vincent Massey
351 St. Joseph Boulevard
HULL, Québec K1A 0H3

Tel.: (819) 997 1360
Fax: (819) 994 6787
Email: filionf@ec.gc.ca

OECD 1999

Canada
Using the Income Tax Act of Canada
to Promote Biodiversity and Sensitive Lands Conservation
Author: Clayton Rubec

Summary: This case study examines recent and proposed changes to the *Canadian Income Tax Act* to promote biodiversity and conservation of ecologically sensitive lands. These were the result of the recommendations of a 1994 Task Force on Economic Instruments and Disincentives to Sound Environmental Practices which deliberated on the incentives and disincentives in the taxation system with regard to conservation of biodiversity. The main recommendations, which were approved in 1996, were to amend the *Act* to exempt from capital gains tax all donations of ecologically sensitive lands made in perpetuity to all levels of government and charities, thus equalising treatment of donations to municipalities and charities with those that are made to the Crown. This allows the use of voluntary, non-regulatory stewardship measures by landowners for biodiversity conservation, encouraged by direct and indirect financial incentives. One of the main conclusions of the 1995 national consultations on the new tax provisions was that there is a need for greater public access to the relevant information.

Ecosystem studied: inland freshwater ecosystems.

Incentive measures used: positive tax incentives.

Main lessons learned: Successful example of the integration of fiscal and environmental policies to encourage conservation of biodiversity on private and corporate-owned lands; co-operation between federal, provincial and non-government partners is essential; and the existence of an appropriate legal context at the provincial level is of great importance.

Contact details of delegate:

Mr. Fernand L. FILION
Director, Environmental Economics Branch
Environment Canada
7th Floor, Place Vincent Massey
351 St. Joseph Boulevard
HULL, Québec K1A 0H3

Tel.: (819) 997 1360
Fax: (819) 994 6787
Email: filionf@ec.gc.ca

Denmark
Economic Incentives for the Transformation
of Privately Cultivated Forest Areas into Strict (Untouched) Forest Reserves
Author: National Nature and Forest Agency, Danish Ministry of Environment and Energy

Summary: This case study examines economic incentives for transforming privately culti-vated forests into strict forest reserves, in accordance with the political goal to double the forested area of Denmark (to 22 per cent) over a 100 year period. Because it was believed to be important to include both public and private lands, the 1994 Danish National Strategy for Natural Forests mandated the increase in forest reserves on public lands, provides grants for reforestation, and offers economic compensation for the voluntary conversion of private for-ests to strict reserves. Indirect compensation is also given to state-owned forests. The Strat-egy also includes plans for research programmes, conservation of local genetic resources, and the dissemination of information to foresters, forest users and the general public. An adverse incentive in the form of a regulation which made it illegal to leave major productive forest areas unproductive was also reformed in 1989 to allow exceptions.

Ecosystem studied: forests.

Incentive measures used: voluntary conservation with compensation, removal of adverse incentives, scientific and technical capacity building.

Main lessons learned: The success of the incentive measure was linked to the fact that it was both voluntary on the part of the landowners and that compensation was offered to them for creating the untouched forest areas.

Contact details of delegate:

Mr. Christian PRIP
Division of Ecology
The National Forest and Nature Agency
Haraldsgade 53
DK-2100 COPENHAGEN

Tel.: (45 39) 472 000
Fax: (45 39) 279 899
Email: CHP@sks.dk

Finland
The Act of the Financing
of Sustainable Forestry and the Development of Forest Certification
Author: Arto Naskali

Summary: This case study discusses the design of a national forest certification scheme in Finland and the effects on sustainable forestry practices there. The Finnish regulatory framework for forestry management has been entirely reformed in recent years, from encouraging intensification (through, for example, subsidies to production and exports) to encouraging environmentally sustainable production. These changes were brought about under the 1994 Environmental Programme for Forestry and the new Forest Act and special Financing of Sustainable Forestry Act in 1997. In addition to removing some of the adverse subsidies, the Financing of Sustainable Forestry Act also provides for the discretionary payment of environmental subsidies to landowners where necessary. A broad-based group formed in 1996 designed a voluntary forest certification scheme (to be operational from 1998) that was compatible with international schemes but reflected the particular circumstances found in Finland.

Ecosystem studied: forests.

Incentive measures used: market creation through certification, removal of adverse incentives, positive subsidies.

Main lessons learned: The implementation of forest certification schemes is facilitated by its market-orientation; because of international trade in forest products, national forest certification schemes should be compatible with international ones; and developing a suitable forest certification system and approval system requires wide-ranging stakeholder involvement (including forest owners and NGOs).

Contact details of delegate:

Mr. Arto NASKALI
Finnish Forest Research Institute
Rovaniemi Research Station
P.O. Box 16
FIN-96301 ROVANIEMI

Tel.: (358) 16 3364 303
Fax: (358) 16 3364 640
Email: arto.naskali@metla.fi

France
A Cost-Benefit Analysis
of Biodiversity Conservation Programmes in the Garonne Valley
Authors: Jean-Pierre Amigues and Brigitte Desaigues

Summary: For this case study, a cost benefit analysis was conducted of a hypothetical plan for biodiversity conservation in the Garonne Valley in France, where the wetlands adjacent to the Garonne river are under pressure from agriculture through erosion and irrigation. Partly this is the result of a property rights problem, as the State is responsible for the river itself and the "regularly flooded areas" around it but, because of the movements of the river bed, these regularly flooded areas are not always easy to determine and the State responsibility for them is rarely enforced. Contingent valuation studies were used to elicit values from farmers of their willingness-to-accept (WTA) compensation for cessation of activities on the river banks which were harmful to biodiversity, and the willingness-to-pay (WTP) values of local residents for these measures. It was found that the WTP value over 5 years would cover a compensation programme of 25 years. However, while this indicates that the estimated benefits of conservation largely exceed the costs, problems with the implementation of incentives were identified. In particular, there was much mistrust between the local residents, farmers and the public authorities.

Ecosystem studied: inland freshwater ecosystems, arable lands.

Incentive measures used: economic valuation, compensation for use restrictions, adverse invectives, positive subsidies, capacity building.

Main lessons learned: The study highlights the need for community participation, awareness raising, and mutual trust and understanding between all relevant parties in the use of contingent valuation (CV) studies, as well as the importance of the policy-making context. The existence of significant scientific information about the pressures in this case was extremely useful.

Contact details of delegate:

M. Bernard GUIBERT
Bureau des Affaires Economiques – DGAD
Ministère de l'Environnement
20 Avenue de Ségur
75302 PARIS

Tel.: (33-1) 42 19 17 21
Fax: (33-1) 42 19 17 71
Email: bernard.guibert@environnement.gouv

OECD 1999

Germany
UNESCO Biosphere Reserves Schorfheide-Chorin and Rhön
Author: Dieter Popp

Summary: This case study examines two German biosphere reserves which are designed to conserve genetic diversity while being sustainably used in an economically viable manner. Visitor fees are charged in the Rhön Reserve and a conservation or exploitation levy has also been proposed. One-quarter of the DM 40 000 generated in visitor fees in 1997 were used for advertising and information awareness campaigns, including supporting the marketing of lamb meat from regenerating stocks in the Reserve. This has now been a success and the scheme is economically viable. In addition, plants in the Reserve are also being tested for medicinal and spice markets. The Schorfheide-Chorin Reserve pays a premium per bee hive to keep apiculture going there and emphasised the necessity of supporting the marketing of products from the Reserves, perhaps through a national campaign and common logo. The importance of a concrete legal framework for the conservation and sustainable use of plant genetic resources and the need to adapt the Commercial Seeds Act were also discussed.

Ecosystems studied: forests, grasslands.

Incentive measures used: access restrictions, regulations, visitor fees, proposed conservation or exploitation levy, legal capacity building, market creation.

Main lessons learned: Public awareness of the benefits of conserving genetic diversity is a strong pre-requisite for achieving this conservation; a combination of instruments should be used to capture the mix of values represented by genetic diversity; consumers are willing to pay higher prices for higher quality or for products from a well-defined regional origin; and appropriate labelling and marketing is required for biodiversity-friendly products to facilitate consumer purchasing.

Contact details of delegate:

Ms. Jessica SUPLIE
Bundesministerium für Umwelt, Naturschutz und Reaktorsicherheit
Godesberger Allee 90
D-53177 BONN

Tel.: (49 228) 305 26 15
Fax: (49 228) 305 26 94
Email: 106023.3672@CompuServe.com

Greece
Incentives for the Conservation of the Nesting Grounds
of the Sea Turtle *Caretta caretta* in Laganas Bay, Zakynthos, Greece
Authors: Stavroula Spyropoulou and Dimitrios Dimopoulos

Summary: This case study describes the range of incentives developed between 1980 and 1997 for the conservation of the nesting grounds of the endangered sea turtle *Caretta caretta* in Laganas Bay, Zakynthos, Greece. The incentives used included regulations and access restrictions (the creation of a Nature Reserve and a planned National Marine Park, as well as restrictions on beach activities, building, fishing, marine traffic and airport operations), the grant-aided purchase of some of the land by the World Wildlife Fund with EU support, information and awareness campaigns (including the employment of local wardens for safeguarding the turtle nests and providing information), and the provision of physical infrastructure (cages) for the protection of the nests. In addition, adverse incentives were identified such as a provision in the 1982 Development Law which encourages the almost unconditional development of new hotels; the lack of verification and enforcement for the payment of the tax on tourism; and property rights uncertainties and disputes that arose as a result of the loss of all ownership records in the 1953 earthquake.

Ecosystem studied: coastal zones.

Incentive measures used: regulations, access restrictions, definition of property rights, removal of adverse incentives, positive subsidies, information provision, capacity building, stakeholder involvement, planned visitor fees.

Main lessons learned: Land use regulations and restrictions have been fairly effective in safeguarding the most sensitive lands, but they are insufficient alone and should be combined with other economic and informational incentives; incentive measures need to be compatible with each other; stakeholder involvement is essential for raising local awareness about biodiversity issues and working towards sustainable use of resources.

Contact details of delegate:

Mr. Dimitri ANDREOU
Permanent Delegation of Greece to the OECD
Hellenic Republic
15 Villa Said   Tel.: (33-1) 45 02 24 00
75116 PARIS   Fax: (33-1) 45 00 71 55

OECD 1999

Japan
The Case of Oze Area: Case Study on the Japanese Experience Concerning Economic Aspects of Conserving Biodiversity
Author: Planning Division, Nature Conservation Bureau, Environment Agency

Summary: This case study describes the conservation measures in use in the Oze National Park in Japan, a primarily marshlands area with some lakes and ponds. The Park is run as a not-for-profit concern and is partly owned by a private company (60 per cent) and partly by the national government (40 per cent). Tourism activities exert the main pressures on biodiversity in the park. There are restrictions on the use of some areas (and boardwalks are provided to protect sensitive, heavy-use areas), on lodge sizes and capacity, and on traffic volumes during peak season. There are also various voluntary measures – such as a voluntary fee for toilet use, a voluntary restriction on shampoo use, a "trash carry home" campaign and a suggested no bathe day. In 1995 a trust fund was established under the Oze Conservation Foundation with 1.4 billion yen per annum (half from public and half from private sources) for the purposes of undertaking educational and institutional building work as well as making management decisions for the Park. Conservation efforts have benefited form the high national profile of Oze National Park, including through its representation in a popular cultural song and a national figure who fought for its conservation.

Ecosystems studied: inland freshwater ecosystems, forests.

Incentive measures used: access and facility restrictions, removal of adverse incentives, environmental fund, education, information provision, voluntary restrictions and fee payments.

Main lessons learned: The co-operation of government bodies, private owners, and environmental NGOs is essential; public awareness and media interest in biodiversity issues can be important tools for facilitating the realisation of conservation objectives, especially on private lands.

Contact details of delegate:

Mr. Taichi ONO
Deputy Director,
Planning Division, Nature Conservation Bureau Environment Agency
1-2-2 Kasumigaseki,
Chiyoda-ku,
TOKYO 100

Tel.: (81-3) 3580-1709
Fax: (81-3) 3591-3228
Email: taichi_ono@eanet.go.jp

Korea
Korean Experiences Relating to the Conservation
of Biodiversity in Mount Chiri, with Special Attention to the Poaching of Bears
Authors: Hio Jung Shin and Hee Man Shon

Summary: This case study discusses measures to protect the extremely endangered Asiatic black bear population in Mount Chiri National Park. The bear numbers had been severely reduced by poaching activities for the use of their gallbladders in traditional Chinese medicine. The bear was designated as a 'national monument' in 1986, the area was classified as a National Park in 1967, and an ambitious protection programme was launched in 1996. This includes bans on the poaching of the bear (with the fines and enforcement levels having recently been sharply increased), controls on the hiking routes and local gun shops, development restrictions in the Park, the removal of subsidies which encourage destruction of the bear habitat, provision of an eco-corridor for easy movement of the bears, and the hiring of ex-poachers to patrol the area. A contingent valuation study revealed a willingness-to-pay for the preservation of the bear species amongst the Korean people of US$ 380 million per bear, while their market value is US$ 67-133 thousand each. Because the bear is such a popular animal in Korea, education and awareness campaigns were also identified as important incentive measures for its protection.

Ecosystem studied: forests, mountainous regions.

Incentive measures used: access restrictions, regulations, fines, stakeholder involvement, removal of adverse incentives, information provision.

Main lessons learned: The involvement of local communities and the support of the media is important, as is the demonstrated will of the government to punish poachers (enforcement of regulations); and an integrated approach to government management of the problem is necessary, with full inter-agency co-operation.

Contact details of delegate:

Mr. Seung-Joon YOON
Permanent Delegation of Korea to the OECD
2/4, rue Louis David
75782 PARIS CEDEX 16

Tel.: 01 44 05 20 59
Fax: 01 47 55 86 70
Email: sjyoon@club_internet.fr

OECD 1999

Mexico
Incitations économiques pour la protection des espèces de la vie sauvage au Mexique: Le cas de l'espèce *Ovis canadensis*
Author: SEMARNAP

Summary: This case study examines economic incentive measures for the protection of the wild big-horned sheep *Ovis canadensis*, which lives in the mountainous arid and semi-arid areas in the north-west of Mexico. There are two principal types of threat to the sheep: general degradation of its habitat and the ecosystem it lives in though, for example, urban development or agricultural expansion; and the more specific, often illegal, activities of individuals which impact on it such as hunting, collection of wild flowers, introduction of exotic species, etc. To permanently stop the process of degradation, a solution is needed which provides new economic alternatives for the local people whose current activities lead to these pressures. It was found that the imposition of regulations alone, without proper monitoring and local community participation, are insufficient. One proposed solution is to give marketable permits for hunting the sheep to the local community, who can then sell these on the international market. This will provide a source of income for the local populations and give them an incentive to ensure hunting is kept at a sustainable level in order to maximise these incomes over time.

Ecosystems studied: arid and semi-arid mountain areas.

Incentive measures used: tradable hunting permits, stakeholder involvement, regulations, information provision, capacity building.

Main lessons learned: Issuing tradable permits to local populations can allow current populations to realise direct value from use of the species as well as providing an incentive for its continued existence for use by future generations (sustainable use); the incentive measures must be well-integrated into other social and institutional frameworks.

Contact details of delegate:

Mr. Germán GONZALEZ-DAVILA
Permanent Representative of the Minister of Environment
4, rue Galliéra, 1st floor
75116 PARIS

Tel.: (33-1) 5367 8618
Fax: (33-1) 4720 0791
Email: germang@world-net.sct.fr

Netherlands
Green Investment Funds: Organic Farming

Authors: Theo van Bellegem, Anne-Marie Beijerman, Arthur Eijs,
M. Boxtel, C. Graveland, and H. Wieringa

Summary: This case study examines how the innovative tax exemption on investments in green funds in place in the Netherlands since January 1995 is utilised to support organic farming there. In general, it was found that the economic gains from organic farming in the Netherlands were low, while the risks were high. The special tax exemption on incomes from investments in approved green funds can help alleviate this and close the profitability gap between traditional and organic production. It allows investors in these projects to contract loans at reduced interest rates (usually about 2 per cent less than commercial rates), providing a financial advantage to organic farms over traditional ones. The funds have been heavily supported by the Dutch people. Other incentives which would also help were identified as the removal of various adverse subsidies to traditional agricultural practices, raising public awareness about organic farming, the development and use of a certified eco-labelling scheme for organic produce, and the imposition of the Polluter Pays Principal to agriculture.

Ecosystem studied: arable lands.

Incentive measures used: positive tax incentives, removal of adverse incentives, market creation, information provision.

Main lessons learned: Successful example of the integration of fiscal and environmental policies; found to be particularly popular with investors; has had a positive effect on the conservation of biodiversity in the Netherlands through encouraging organic farming; however, a very precise definition of the criteria used to define "green" practices was essential.

Contact details of delegates:

Mr. Arthur EIJS
Ministry of Housing, Physical Planning and Environment, ipc 655
Rijnstraat 8
P.O. Box 30945
2500 GX THE HAGUE

Tel.: (31 70) 339 46 96
Fax: (31 70) 339 12 97
Email: A.Eijs@DSVS.DGM.minvrom.nl

Mr. Theo Van BELLEGEM
Ministry of Housing, Physical Planning and Environment, ipc 660
Rijnstraat 8
P. O. Box 30945
2500 GX THE HAGUE

Tel.: (31) 70 339 4089
Fax: (31) 70 339 1304
Email: Vanbellegem@DB.DGM.minvrom.nl

Netherlands
Green Investment Funds: PIM Project

Authors: Theo van Bellegem, Anne-Marie Beijerman, and Arthur Eijs

Summary: This case study examines the Project Infiltration Maaswater (PIM) in the Netherlands to limit desiccation caused by the lowering of the water table through excessive groundwater abstraction. The PIM project is an initiative of a drinking-water supply company to change from using groundwater to purified and filtered surface water. However, ground-water abstraction is more economically viable than this treatment at current prices. In order to alleviate the environmental pressures caused by groundwater use, the Dutch government is using a number of measures to help to close the profitability gap between these two alternatives in order to make the treatment of surface water a more viable option. First, the PIM project is being financially supported – partly through EU funds and partly by the Dutch government through their classification of it as a green project so that investments in green funds which support it can be exempt from tax. Second, most provinces have introduced ground-water extraction levies, and the central government has also been taxing water extraction since 1995. Third, permits are now required for groundwater abstraction and only a limited number are available in most provinces. Finally, groundwater abstractions will be completely abolished or reduced in three locations.

Ecosystem studied: inland freshwater ecosystems.

Incentive measures used: positive tax incentives, market creation, information provision, capacity building.

Main lessons learned: The scheme has been very effective in supporting the PIM project; it is equitable in that it applies to all green funds, and is limited to those with only moderate profits; it requires only a fairly simple administrative system; it is popular with banks, project owners and the public; however, the scheme is not sufficient on its own, but should be a part of an integrated approach to the biodiversity pressures which utilises a mix of incentive measures.

Contact details of delegates:

Mr. Arthur EIJS
Ministry of Housing, Physical Planning and Environment, ipc 655
Rijnstraat 8
P.O. Box 30945
2500 GX THE HAGUE

Tel.: (31 70) 339 46 96
Fax: (31 70) 339 12 97
Email: A.Eijs@DSVS.DGM.minvrom.nl

Mr. Theo Van BELLEGEM
Ministry of Housing, Physical Planning and Environment, ipc 660
Rijnstraat 8
P. O. Box 30945
2500 GX THE HAGUE

Tel.: (31) 70 339 4089
Fax: (31) 70 339 1304
Email: Vanbellegem@DB.DGM.minvrom.nl

New Zealand
Conservation of the Pae O Te Rangi Area
Author: Gerard Hutching

Summary: This case study examines the joint purchase in 1993 of forested lands in the Pae O Te Rangi area by the New Zealand government's heritage fund and two local authorities for conversion into a reserve. Previously, the lands had been privately owned by a Maori tribe and large areas had been logged and converted to sheep and cattle farming and horticultural uses. These activities were encouraged up until 1984 by direct subsidies for land clearance and agricultural market price support, as well as tax disincentives and support to road infrastructure. However, in recent years the property was no longer economically viable as a farm and there was an intention to subdivide it into small blocks to sell for development purposes. In order to prevent this, and under pressure from local interest groups, the land was purchased for conversion into a reserve instead. Stakeholders were involved in the process, and the plans were supported by the Maori tribe who previously owned the lands. In 1990 a Forest Heritage Fund was created to support the voluntary undertaking of sustainable forestry practices on private lands with compensation offered to those who are no longer allowed to log.

Ecosystem studied: forests.

Incentive measures used: property purchase, access restrictions, adverse incentives removal, environmental fund.

Main lessons learned: Dealings with private land owners must be fair and transparent; NGOs can be useful in identifying areas for protection and pressuring key players to protect them; it can help to use a third party (outside of local authority) to purchase the land if negotiations are difficult; the development of strict criteria for forest purchases by independent bodies is necessary.

Contact details of delegate:

Ms Joanna KEMPKERS
Second Secretary
New Zealand Permanent Delegation
7ter, rue Léonard-de-Vinci
75116 PARIS

Tel.: (33-1) 4500 2411 E.262
Fax: (33-1) 4501 2639

OECD 1999

Norway
Valuation of Benefits Connected to Conservation or Improvement of Environmental Quality in Local Watercourses in Norway

Authors: Kristin Magnussen and Espen Rymoen

Summary: For this case study, a valuation was conducted of the benefits associated with undertaking programmes to ensure the conservation or improvement of environmental quality in two Norwegian waterways. The benefits were estimated using contingent valuation studies informed by expert panels, and they included the benefits from improved water quality, recreation and biodiversity. The main pressures on the waterways are high nutrient levels which stem from municipal waste water and agriculture, with some large discharges of nitrogen from industrial point sources. Development and land clearance on the banks of the rivers was also identified as a pressure on the water quality. Compensation is currently offered to landowners or farmers for creating a new field or river margin, and 41 per cent of farmland is now set-aside, but this has not been as effective as hoped because it does not target erosion-prone lands. Restrictions on development and the provision of better sewage treatment facilities were also recommended. The study emphasised in particular the need to develop holistic programmes for managing the waterways and the importance of public education and participation of local residents in these programmes.

Ecosystem studied: inland freshwater ecosystems.

Incentive measures used: economic valuation, regulations, positive subsidies.

Main lessons learned: Significant variations in WTP values were found for different rivers (so these results are not transferable); non-use values of the waterways were found to be particularly high; a range of measures for providing information, building capacity and involving stakeholders should be used; and undertaking WTP studies can be costly and time-consuming.

Contact details of delegate:

Mr. Finn KATERAAS (Vice-Chairman)
Directorate for Nature Management
N-7005 TRONDHEIM

Tel.: (47 73) 58 08 30
Fax: (47 73) 58 05 01
Email: finn.kateras@dn.dep.no

Poland
The Implementation of Economic Incentive Measures to Promote the Conservation and Sustainable Use of Biodiversity in the Biebrza Valley, with Special Attention to the Biebrza National Park

Author: Ministry of Environmental Protection, Natural Resources and Forestry

Summary: This case study examines measures to protect a peatland swamp in Poland, part of which falls within the Biebrza National Park. Because of a lack of tourism opportunities, there are no incentives for the local population to conserve biodiversity in the area. Similarly, because of low government financial resources in the region, there is little opportunity for financial support to promote environmentally-friendly activities. The lack of an appropriate legal and regulatory framework for reclaiming or protecting the peatlands was identified. One of the main difficulties identified in the study is that the river catchment extends beyond the boundaries of the Park, so activities undertaken outside the Park have strong effects on the river quality and flow. These include water abstraction for irrigation purposes and the destruction of forests around the park, the latter of which have increased in recent years with the removal of a requirement to hold a permit to undertake these activities. The most promising solutions suggested in the study included the use of debt-for-nature ecofunds to support conservation activities and the development of eco-tourism activities in the region to generate a self-funding conservation programme.

Ecosystems studied: inland freshwater ecosystems.

Incentive measures used: charges, permits, access restrictions, tax reforms, environmental fund, education and information provision, regulatory reform.

Main lessons learned: Conservation activities in the park need to be properly integrated with national and local economic objectives; the use of environmental funds, including from foreign sources, is particularly useful where government finances are limited.

Contact details of delegate:

Mr. Zygmunt KRZEMINSKI
Deputy Director
Nature Protection Department
Ministry of Environmental Protection, Natural Resources and Forestry
Wawelska 52-54   Tel.: (48-22) 256 204
WARSAW 00922   Fax: (48-22) 254 705
Email: zkrzemin@mos.gov.pl

OECD 1999

Turkey
The Development of Appropriate Methods for Community Forestry in Turkey

Authors: Suade Arançli and Peter R. Stevens

Summary: This case study examines practical methods for developing community forestry programmes in 20 forest villages in Turkey. This approach was found to be necessary because the government was unable to sufficiently enforce and monitor restrictions on illegal poaching, tree felling and agricultural activities which had resulted in infertile, eroded soils and steep landscapes. Essentially, conflicts arose between the government plans to protect the forest areas and the needs of the local villagers to earn sufficient income from the forest to survive. Thus, it was decided that the institutional structure needed to be reformed to allow for co-management of the forest by the villagers and the government, and participatory rural appraisals of the developments. Practical training sessions have been provided for villagers to help develop methods for sustainably using the forests while still generating sufficient income for the villages. These have been largely successful, and the next stage will be to expand the education programme to look at the up- and down-stream effects of different activities.

Ecosystem studied: forests.

Incentive measures used: practical training and information provision, stakeholder involvement, positive subsidies, institutional reform.

Main lessons learned: Local community participation and the use of integrated natural resource management techniques are important; community forestry projects which encourage the sustainable and profitable use of forest resources and increase awareness in local villages and with foresters, result in significant environmental improvements, and help to coordinate catchment-level activities.

Contact details of delegates:

Ms. Ergül TERZIOGLU
Directorate of Environmental Protection
Ministry of the Environment
ANKARA

Tel.: (31 2) 287 99 63/24 07
Fax: (31 2) 286 22 71

Ms. Yonca GÜNDÜZ-OZCERI
Permanent Delegation of Turkey to the OECD
9 Rue Alfred-Dehodencq
75116 Paris

Tel.: (33 1) 42 88 50 02
Fax: (33 1) 45 27 28 24

United Kingdom
Heathland Management in the UK
Authors: David Harley and Robert C. Davies

Summary: This case study describes existing and potential incentive measures for the management of lowland heathlands in Dorset. Under the UK Biodiversity Action Plan, all existing lowland heathland is to be maintained, and a further 6 000 hectares is to be established by the year 2005. In the past, agricultural subsidies encouraged the conversion from heathlands, but today they are used to encourage the re-creation of the heathlands. Under the EU Agri-Environmental Regulation there are payments to private land managers to conserve heathlands. In addition, three projects on the Dorset Heathlands have been supported through environmental funds established through landfill tax credits. The study also suggested the possible use of a quarrying tax and/ or a greenfield development levy to counter urban sprawl and raise funds for brownfield redevelopment. There are also possible new markets which can be realised through sustainable use of the heathlands, such as the production of organic, extensively-reared meat or the generation of renewable energy through the burning of the by-products of heathland management (*e.g.* gorse). The RSPB Dorset Heathland Project undertakes practical conservation measures (largely based on voluntary field staff), and trains other groups or individuals in the sustainable management of the heathlands.

Ecosystem studied: arid and semi-arid areas.

Incentive measures used: Training and information provision, agri-environmental subsidies, market creation, environmental levies and taxes.

Main lessons learned: Public and private sector initiatives need to be co-ordinated; conservation initiatives should be comprehensive and wide-ranging; national and EU policies must be integrated; and new markets should be identified and established for long-term sustainable use of heathlands.

Contact details of delegate:

Mr. Robert C. DAVIES
Economic Adviser
Central Economics and Policy Division
Department of the Environment, Transport and the Regions
Floor 4/25B, Great Minster House   Tel.: (44 171) 890 3620
76 Marsham Street   Fax: (44 171)676 2178
LONDON SW1P 4DR   Email: bdavies@cedoce.demon.co.uk

United States
US Experiences with Incentive Measures
to Promote the Conservation of Wetlands

Authors: Ralph Heimlich, Keith Wiebe, Roger Claassen and Dwight Gadsby

Summary: This case study describes the incentive measures used in the US to conserve wetlands. For many years, various support measures were in place which contributed to the destruction of wetlands in the US, including direct subsidies for wetland drainage, market price support for agricultural products, tax incentives for purchasing wetland draining machinery, and other government assistance for draining wetlands or agricultural expansion and production. While most of these have been removed, they contributed to the conversion of nearly half the wetlands in the US to other uses since 1780. In addition to the removal of these adverse subsidies, positive incentive measures have also been developed for the conservation of wetlands. These include the purchase by government bodies of wetlands for protection purposes or agricultural lands for the restoration of wetlands, and the establishment of subsidies for conservation activities.

Ecosystem studied: inland freshwater ecosystems.

Incentive measures used: government purchase, removal of adverse incentives, positive subsidies, information provision, scientific capacity building, institution building.

Main lessons learned: Public sentiment evolves in relation to wetlands according to their scarcity and the relative needs for economic development, but can be influenced by education and dissemination of scientific knowledge; it is often necessary to use a variety of incentives to address the variety of pressures and their settings; each type of policy is costly in its own way – politically, legally, financially, etc.; an important role is played by the reform of subsidies which encouraged the draining of wetlands.

Contact details of delegate:

Mr. Joseph FERRANTE (Chairman)
United States Environmental Protection Agency
Office of Policy Analysis (2121A)   Tel.: (202) 260 2790
401 M. St. NW   Fax: (202) 260 2300
WASHINGTON, D.C. 20460   Email: ferrante.joe@epamail.epa.gov

OECD

Individual Transferable Quotas as an Incentive Measure
for the Conservation and the Sustainable Use of Marine Biodiversity

Authors: Eyjo Gudmundsson, Jan Horst Keppler and Jon Sutinen

Summary: This case study discusses the use of individual transferable quotas (ITQs) for the conservation and sustainable use of marine biodiversity. When total allowable catches (TACs) are established for commercial fisheries, the rights to fish can be allocated through ITQs which allow the holder to fish a certain proportion of the TAC. These essentially define property rights over the resources, allowing the maximisation of privately appropriable resource rents. The study emphasised that other complementary measures may be required as well to achieve the desired conservation aims, including regulations specifying minimum mesh size, conditions pertaining to gear and vessels, or limits on the number of days at sea; the reduction of subsidies to production, infrastructure and vessels, and the removal of barriers to trade; vessel buy-back programmes; incentives to conserve and sustainably use the surrounding ecosystem and particularly non-commercial species; and – as a final resort – moratoriums on overfished fisheries. In addition, it was found that ITQs work best in small, isolated fisheries where there is some social cohesion and where education and re-training programmes are offered if necessary. It is essential to gain the co-operation and active participation of the involved fishers.

Ecosystem studied: marine ecosystems.

Incentive measures used: individual transferable quotas (ITQs, total allowable catches (TACs), regulations, access restrictions, removal of adverse incentives, positive subsidies, stakeholder involvement.

Main lessons learned: ITQs should be applied in combination with other incentive measures (gear restrictions to reduce by-catch, community involvement, limitations on time and space of fishing etc.) to overcome their main limitation, *i.e.*, the fact that their effectiveness is restricted to the commercial target species; the sale or taxation of quotas generates revenues which can be used to finance research, monitoring and enforcement of the schemes and also to compensate for undesired social impacts such as a reduction of employment opportunities.

Contact details:

Jan Horst KEPPLER
Economics Division, Environment Directorate
OECD
2 rue André-Pascal
75775 PARIS CEDEX 16

Tel.: 01 45 24 19 47
Fax: 01 45 24 78 76
Email: jan.keppler@oecd.org

Annex 3

Glossary of Important Terms

Access restrictions: a measure to conserve biodiversity through restricting access to geographical areas or to the biological resources themselves. Particularly common in situations where there is an endangered species or ecosystem requiring protection for which no level of use is sustainable. (V.1; V.2; VII.2)

Adverse/ perverse incentives: any incentive which induces behaviour that lead to a reduction in biological diversity; they are the result of government intervention failures. (V.1; V.2; V.3; VII.1)

Assignment of property rights: the delineation of the rights of individuals or the public to biological or environmental goods or components of them – to use or trade them, or to exclude others from their use. (IV.1; V.1; V.2; V.3; VII.1)

Benefit sharing: the fair and equitable sharing of the benefits arising from the use of biological resources, especially genetic resources, between providers of the resource and those who transform or commercialise them. (IV.1; IV.3)

Benefits transfer: the process by which monetary valuations of the benefits of environmental resources (or the costs associated with their loss) can be applied to other, similar situations. (VI.1; VII.3)

Bequest values: the value humans place on ecosystems or biological resources for the possibility of maintaining them for the use or enjoyment by future generations. (IV.1)

Biodiversity prospecting: the search for potentially valuable biochemical or genetic resources as mediated through contractual agreements between the owners of genetic resources and others interested in access to those genetic resources (usually pharmaceutical firms). (VII.1)

Biological diversity: the variability among living organisms from all sources including, *inter alia*, terrestrial, marine and other aquatic ecosystems and the ecological complexities of which they are part; this includes diversity within species, between species and of ecosystems (CBD, 1994). (IV.1)

Biological resources: genetic resources, organisms or parts thereof, populations, or any other biotic components of ecosystems with actual or potential use or value for humanity (CBD, 1994). (V)

Clearing-House Mechanism: a facility established by the Conference of the Parties to the Convention on Biological Diversity to ensure that information and experiences are shared among interested parties. (VII.3)

Club good: a good that is not private, but whose use is exclusive to a certain group of people (non-rival, but exclusive). (VI.1)

Conference of the Parties to the Convention on Biological Diversity: represents the Contracting Parties to the Convention; it is responsible for taking decisions on implementing and monitoring the progress of the Convention. (III)

Conservation: the implementation of measures to ensure that biodiversity resources are used, managed and protected such that there is the absence of a decline in biodiversity. (IV.3; V.1; V.3; VII.1; VII.2; VII.3)

Contingent valuation studies: derives economic valuations for environmental goods or services through surveying people directly to find what they are willing to pay for a biodiversity benefit and/or what they are willing to accept in compensation for the removal of such a benefit. (VII.3)

Convention on Biological Diversity (CBD): an international convention signed by 150 nations at the Earth Summit in Rio de Janeiro in 1992 which entered into force in December 1993; its aims are the conservation of biodiversity, the sustainable use of its components, and the equitable sharing of its benefits; ratified by over 160 countries and the European Union by the end of 1996. (III.3; IV.3)

Covenants: see *Easements.*

Creation of markets: the removal of barriers to trade and the assignment of well-defined property rights to create markets where environmental goods and services with privately-appropriable values can be traded to realise their full potential values. Generates incentives for the sustainable use of resources. (V.1; V.2; V.3; VII.1)

Debt-for-nature swaps: the purchase of a country's debt at a discount on the secondary market and its redemption in return for environmental conservation action on the part of the debtor government. (VII.2)

Direct use values: the value to human societies of those elements of biodiversity which can be directly consumed, traded or used as an input to commercial activities. (IV.1; VII.1)

Easements: contractual agreements between private land users or owners and public or non-governmental organisations which commit the landowners to undertake specified conservation or sustainable use practices on the land. Agreements are often voluntary and accompanied by some financial compensation. (V.2; VII.1)

Eco-labelling: the provision of information about product characteristics that relate to the environment to enable more informed consumer purchasing decisions and to differentiate products for the creation of separate markets for the differentiated products. (V.2; V.3; VI.2 ; VII.1; VII.3)

Ecological threshold: a level of biodiversity deterioration beyond which the ecosystem will experience a sudden increase in adverse and possibly irreversible effects on the system's functioning and overall resilience to change. (III.2; IV.1; VII.4)

Economic valuation: the assignment of monetary values for environmental goods and services for which market values do not exist, so that these values can be explicitly reflected in any decision-making process based on monetary benefits and costs. (VII.1; VII.3)

Ecosystem approach: the tackling of biodiversity conservation or sustainable use through the use of measures which address the whole ecosystem, rather than a focus on its individual components. (V)

Ecosystem: a dynamic complex of plant, animal and micro-organism communities and their non-living environment interacting as a functional unit (CBD, 1994). (IV.3; V)

Ecosystem services/indirect use values: all those functions of the environment which provide direct value to the well-being of humans through the maintenance of a healthy environment, *e.g.* flood control, water purification, soil maintenance. (IV.1; VII.3)

Eco-tourism: tourism which creates private revenues without destroying the underlying public asset of attractive ecosystems (sustainable use); can provide a safeguard against competing pressures for land use change, agricultural expansion, etc. (IV.3; V.1)

Environmental fees and user charges: compulsory, requited fees for the use of an environmental good or service. A good or service is provided in exchange for the fee or charge. These generate revenue that can be recycled to biodiversity conservation, and increase the private cost of resource use. (V.1; V.3; VII.1)

Environmental funds: revenue or resources from public or private sources that are set-aside for use only for specified environmental purposes. (IV.1; VII.2)

Environmental taxes: compulsory, unrequited payments to general government linked to the use of environmental goods and services. Benefits provided by government to taxpayers are not generally in proportion to their payments. These generate revenue that can be recycled to biodiversity conservation, and increase the private cost of resource use. (V.2; VII.1)

Existence values: the value humans place on ecosystems or biological resources for their pure existence. (IV.1; V; VII.1)

Ex-*situ* conservation: the conservation of components of biological diversity outside their natural habitats (CBD, 1994). (IV.3)

Externalities: costs or benefits which result from an activity but accrue to others than those undertaking the activity without any mechanism to impute them to the original actors; the existence of externalities is closely linked to the absence of markets for the goods in question. (IV.2; V.1; V.2; VII.1; VII.3)

Government intervention failure: interventions by government that distort price signals and markets to the detriment of biodiversity. (VII.1)

Habitat: the place or type of site where an organism or population occurs naturally. (V; VII.3)

Hedonic pricing methods: derives economic valuations for environmental goods or services through examining variations in the prices paid for properties which are associated to a greater or lesser degree of the environmental attributes. (VII.3)

159

In-situ conservation: the conservation of ecosystems and natural habitats and the maintenance and recovery of viable populations of species in their natural surroundings and, in the case of domesticated or cultivated species, in the surroundings where they have developed their distinctive properties (CBD, 1994). (IV.3)

Incentive measures: any measure that creates or improves upon the available markets and price signals for biological resources to encourage the conservation or sustainable use of biological diversity (IV.2; V; VI; VII)

Indirect use values: see *ecosystem services.*

Information provision: ensuring relevant scientific and technological information is at the disposal of decision-makers and stakeholders in order to inform government policies and individual decisions about the use of biological resources. (V.1; V.2; V.3; VI.1; VI.2; VII.3)

Institution building: the creation or strengthening of specially designed institutions for mediating, monitoring and enforcing incentive measures for the sustainable management of biodiversity. (V.1; V.2; VII.3)

Institutional capacity: the overall capacity of government, community, and private groups to effectively design, manage, and enforce biodiversity policy. (VI.1; VII.3)

Integration failure: a lack of capacity or institutional structure to adequately take full account of the effects of sectoral policy on biodiversity; *e.g.* the effects of transport policy on biodiversity. (V.2; VI.1)

Intellectual property rights: to promote and protect innovation by allowing the 'owner' of the knowledge to have security over his/ her invention for a designated period of time. (IV.3; VII.1)

Market failure: the failure of the interplay of market forces to secure the economically correct level of biodiversity conservation or sustainable use due to the fact that market prices do not reflect the full value to society of biodiversity. (III.2; VII.1; VII.3))

Option values: the values associated with maintaining biological resources so that choices can be made regarding their use in an uncertain future. (IV.1)

Positive incentives: any monetary or non-monetary inducement which directly incites or motivates governments, local people, or organisations to conserve or sustainably use biological resources, or to equitably share the benefits of their use. (V.1; V.2; V.3: VII.2)

Precautionary approach/principal: an environmental decision-making principle which states that "where there are threats of serious or irreversible damage, lack of full scientific certainty shall not be used as a reason for postponing cost-effective measures to prevent environmental degradation"(Principle 15, Rio Declaration on Environment and Development, 1992). (III.2, IV.1; VI.2)

Private goods or services: goods and services for which one person's consumption depletes its availability to others (rival) and for which it is possible to exclude people from its consumption (exclusivity). (IV.2; V.3; VII.1)

Protected area: a geographically defined area which is designated or regulated and managed to achieve specific conservation objectives (CBD, 1994). (V.3; VII.1; VII.2)

Public goods or services: goods and services whose benefits are not depleted by an additional user (non-rival) and for which it is generally not possible to exclude people from its benefits (non-exclusive). (IV.2; VII.1; VII.3)

Regulations: see *standards and regulations.*

Resilience: a measure of the ability of an ecosystem to withstand stress and shocks; to persist in the face of unpredictable and sometimes drastic natural changes and pressures. (IV)

Safe minimum standards: a biodiversity decision-making principle which suggests that there be a presumption in favour of not harming biodiversity unless the opportunity costs of that action are very high; *i.e.* no significant deterioration of biodiversity should occur unless the benefits associated with that deterioration heavily outweigh the costs of deterioration. (III.2)

Species: a population whose members are able to interbreed freely under natural conditions. (IV)

Stakeholder involvement: the provision of institutional structures for the involvement of representatives of all parties affected by biodiversity or its loss in processes for determining its management. (V.1; V.2; V.3; VI.1; VI.2; VII.3)

Standards and regulations: legal measures which restrict, prohibit or require certain activities or methods or levels of undertaking them. (V.1; V.2; V.3; VII.1; VII.2)

Support measures/subsidies: any government-directed, market-distorting, intervention which decreases the cost of producing a specific good or service, or increases the price which may be charged for that good or service. (V.1; V.2; VII.1; VII.2)

Sustainable use: the use of components of biological diversity in a way and at a rate that does not lead to the long-term decline of biological diversity, thereby maintaining its potential to meet the needs and aspirations of present and future generations (CBD, 1994). (IV.3; VI.2; VII.1; VII.2; VII.4)

Tradable/transferable permits or rights: rights or allowances to undertake a certain restricted activity – such as the emission of pollutants, land development, harvesting of a particular species, etc. – which can be traded between interested parties through a market. (V.1; V.2; V.3; VII.1)

Travel-cost methods: derives economic estimates of people's values for biodiversity resources according to the amount of time and money they are willing to expend to reach the resource. (VII.3)

Use rights: the rights over certain aspects of a natural resource for private uses (*e.g.* bioprospecting, grazing, hunting), which does *not* include the right to sell the resource or to damage the surrounding ecosystem, and may be linked to certain conditions or *covenants* ensuring the sustainability of use. (VII.1)

OECD 1999

Notes

1. This is another one of the five priority activities established by the OECD Secretary-General.

2. Needless to say, further information on the ecological workings of biodiversity as well as its economic values remains extremely helpful for policy making. As implied in the precautionary approach embodied in Principle 15 of the *Rio Declaration on Environment and Development* (United Nations Conference on Environment and Development, 1992), what has to be abandoned is not the search for more information, but the ideal of optimal policy making under complete information and certainty.

3. *Awareness failures* exist where the physical conditions for deterioration are already present, but the impacts have not yet been realised.

4. The term "ecosystem" is defined in Article 2 of the Convention on Biological Diversity as "... a dynamic complex of plant, animal and micro-organism communities and their non-living environment interacting as a functional unit".

5. Somewhat misleadingly, such a situation is sometimes referred to as "the tragedy of the commons". While there is true tragedy in the rapid depletion of natural resources under open access, commonly managed resources, such as the village commons, have often been remarkably successful in avoiding it (see, for instance, Hanna and Munasinghe, 1995).

6. Good introductions to the derivation of environmental values can be found in Barbier (1989), Barde and Pearce (1991), Pearce and Markandya (1989) and Freeman (1993).

7. A recent, not uncontroversial, study estimated the value of all the world's (global and local) ecosystem services as lying in the range of US$ 16-54 trillion (10^{12}) per year (Costanza *et al.*, 1997). This compares to the global value of economic goods and services annually produced of US$ 18 trillion.

8. This is sometimes referred to as the *Victim Pays Principle*, as opposed to the Polluter or User Pays Principles.

9. Article 21 of the Convention on Biological Diversity provides for a mechanism for the provision of financial resources to developing country Parties for the purposes of the Convention on a grant or concessional basis. It was decided at the first meeting of the Conference of Parties to the Convention that the Global Environment Facility (GEF) will continue to serve as the institutional structure to operate the financial mechanism on an interim basis, in accordance with Article 39 of the Convention.

OECD 1999

10. Not all private owners conform to the caricature of the purely self-interested economic agent. Some do indeed contribute consciously and significantly to the realisation of public goods, even at a cost to themselves through a reduction in their profits. Conversely, it is not always the case that government interventions reflect the true public interest.

11. See *Environmental Benefits of Agriculture: Issues and Policies* OECD (1997c) for detailed examples.

12. Such as the Convention to Combat Desertification (1994), the Convention on International Trade in Endangered Species of Wild Fauna and Flora (CITES, 1973), the Convention on Migratory Species of Wild Animals (Bonn Convention, 1983), the Convention on Wetlands (Ramsar Convention, 1971), and the World Heritage Convention (1972).

13. The gap between private profitability and social optimality can be overcome by different instruments: either regulations and prohibitions if property rights lie with the general public, or subsidies and support for sustainable use if the property rights lie with the users of the components of biodiversity. The implicit and explicit allocations of property rights can vary, of course, from case to case.

14. In fact, only one of the case studies (Germany) provided by Member countries for the *Handbook* has included a focus on genetic resources, while three have focused on species and nineteen on ecosystems.

15. The question whether private users of biodiversity or its elements should be obliged to incur the costs of sustainable use or should be compensated for doing so cannot be decided *a priori*. The answer will depend in each case on questions of distributional equity and political feasibility. From an economic point of view, both solutions can be efficient.

16. SBSTTA is the Subsidiary Body on Scientific, Technical and Technological Advice of the Conference of Parties to the Convention on Biological Diversity.

17. Species are considered "endangered" if they are in danger of extinction and if their survival is unlikely if the causal factors leading to their demise continue operating. Species are considered "vulnerable" if they are likely to move into the "endangered" category in the near future if the causal factors continue to operate.

18. High-grading is the practice of discarding the smaller, often young, fish and keeping only the high-grade ones to count against a harvest quota.

19. Note that the typology used in this Chapter divides wetlands between coastal wetlands (Section V.1) and inland wetland ecosystems (Section V.2).

20. It is a priority issue on the agenda for the SBSTTA 4 meeting, held in Montreal, Canada, in June 1999.

21. For more information, see De Civita *et al.*, (1998).

22. At the same time, there also exist management practices used by indigenous or local communities which are detrimental to biodiversity. In such cases, as with all other pressures on biodiversity discussed in this *Handbook*, it may be advantageous to design and implement incentive measures to encourage a move towards more sustainable practices.

23. The incentive measures could be organised in a range of different ways, but this classificatory framework seemed the most comprehensive and logical for the case studies examined. Some of the categories overlap or have strong links with other ones, such that a number of the incentive measures reviewed could readily fit into more than one category. Wherever possible, these links and overlaps have been made transparent in the text.

24. Annex II provides a more comprehensive overview of each case study.

25. Economic incentives derived from a theory of static optimisation under full knowledge are most useful for solving those aspects of biodiversity management which inscribe themselves into the logic of classic natural resource problems, *i.e.* the optimal allocation of a natural resource such as, say, a fishery, with a known private value. Privatisation, permit allocation, or the reflection of negative externalities through an extraction fee or royalty can fully prevent inefficient rent dissipation. The logic of biodiversity conservation, however, frequently has to deal with less clear-cut cases.

26. This concept was first developed by Arthur C. Pigou (1920). Such environmental taxes or charges are therefore also referred to as "Pigovian taxes".

27. The most important techniques available are contingent valuation, hedonic pricing, travel cost measurement cost of substitution with private goods, and benefits transfer (see Pearce *et al.*, 1994).

28. Such as, for example, the Landfill Tax which is applied in the UK with the explicit purpose of internalising the external environmental and social costs of landfill disposal in the private costs of those disposing of the waste.

29. The OECD will continue to explore the effects of removing or reforming environmentally adverse subsidies as one of its focus areas in the horizontal project on sustainable development.

30. The logic is identical to that for taxes and charges with, however, the property rights reversed in this case to lie with landowners rather than with the general public.

31. With respect to environmental funds in non-OECD countries, the OECD published the *St. Petersburg Guidelines on Environmental Funds in the Transition to a Market Economy* in 1995 and a *Survey on Environmental Funds in CEEC and NIS Countries* is forthcoming (OECD, forthcoming 1999c).

32. Unfortunately, it would not be possible to directly copy the Dutch green investment funds scheme in many other countries because it is specific to the tax system used in the Netherlands. However, variations with similar benefits could probably be established.

33. Transaction costs can be considered all the obstacles to arriving at satisfying outcomes and the creation of those feedback mechanisms necessary to overcome the existence of externalities. They include the costs of gathering information, the costs of setting up mechanisms and institutions for evaluating and transmitting the information, as well as the costs of defining, monitoring, adjudicating and enforcing property rights, responsibilities and liabilities.

34. This term is actually a misnomer, as the medieval village commons, which stand at the origin of the expression, were subject to well-defined public property rights and a web of rules and social conventions which regulated their use at a sustainable level. They are, in fact, a good example of overcoming the free-rider issues or the 'tragedy of the commons' in a case in which public provision and maintenance has advantages over private market provision: through the definition and enforcement of public ownership and use rights and the implementation of appropriate incentive measures.

35. Transaction costs of co-ordination are, of course, particularly relevant with regard to global existence values. In these cases, institutional co-ordination of governments is necessary to avoid large-scale policy failures.

36. However, there is a strong probability that the public surveyed actually gave their willingness to pay for a *national* biodiversity programme, not just the programme described for the Garonne Valley.

37. The term "tragedy of the commons" should not be confused with any form of communal property management that precisely fulfils the function to prevent the tragedy of uncontrolled over-exploitation.

38. While a complex economic and policy topic in itself, agri-environmental payments by the European Union to certain groups of its farmers that are willing to comply with sustainable agricultural practices have partly been developed on the basis of the same conceptual approach.

Bibliography

The references to case studies undertaken for this report are all marked with an "".
They are all OECD General Documents, and their full texts are available
at the OECD Internet site at http://www.oecd.org/env/eco*

*AMIGUES, J-P. and DESAIGUES, B. (1999),
"France: A Cost-benefit Analysis of Biodiversity Conservation Programmes in the Garonne Valley".

*ARANÇLI, S. and STEVENS, P. (1999),
"The Development of Appropriate Methods for Community Forestry in Turkey". [Note: this study was originally undertaken in 1995].

ARROW, K.J. and FISHER, A.C. (1974),
"Environmental Preservation, Uncertainty and Irreversibility", *Quarterly Journal of Economics*, 88, pp. 313-319.

BARBIER, E.B. (1989),
The Economic Value of Ecosystems 1: Tropical Wetlands, LEEC Gatekeeper 89-02, London Environmental Economics Centre, London.

BARBIER, E.B. (1994),
"Valuing Environmental Functions: Tropical Wetlands," *Land Economics*, 70(2), pp. 155-173.

BARBIER, E.B., BURGESS, J.C. and FOLKE, C. (1994),
Paradise Lost? The Ecological Economics of Biodiversity, Earthscan Publications Ltd, London.

BARBIER, E.B., MARKANDYA, A. and PEARCE, D.W. (1990),
"Environmental Sustainability and Cost-Benefit Analysis", *Environment and Planning*, A 22, pp. 1259-1266.

BARDE, J-P. AND PEARCE, D.W. (eds.) (1991),
Valuing the Environment: Six Case Studies, Earthscan Publications, London.

*BELLEGEM, T. VAN, BEIJERMAN, A. and EIJS, A. (1999*a*),
"Green Investment Funds: PIM Project".

*BELLEGEM, T. VAN, BEIJERMAN, A., EIJS, A., BOXTEL, M., GRAVELAND, C. and WIERINGA, H. (1999*b*),
"Green Investment Funds: Organic Farming".

BROOKES, M. (1998),
"The Species Enigma", in *New Scientist*, No. 111, June, pp. 1-4.

BROOKSHIRE, D.S. and NEILL, H.R. (1992),
"Benefit Transfers: Conceptual and Empirical Issues", in *Water Resources Research*, 28 (3).

*CARTER, M. (1999),
"A Revolving Fund for Biodiversity Conservation in Australia".

COMMONWEALTH OF AUSTRALIA (1996),
The National Strategy for the Conservation of Australia's Biological Diversity, Commonwealth Department of Environment, Sport and Territories, Canberra.

CONFERENCE OF PARTIES TO THE CONVENTION ON BIOLOGICAL DIVERSITY (1996),
"Sharing of Experiences on Incentive Measures for Conservation and Sustainable Use" (Document UNEP/CBD/COP/3/24), UNEP, Buenos Aires.

COSTANZA, R., D'ARGE, R., DE GROOT, R., FARBER, S., GRASSO, M., HANNON, B., LIMBURG, K., NAEEM, S., O'NEILL, R.V., PARUELO, J., RASKIN, R., SUTTON, P. and MARJAN VAN DER BELT (1997),
"The Value of the World's Ecosystem Services and Natural Capital", in *Nature* 387, May, pp. 253-260.

*DANISH MINISTRY OF ENVIRONMENT AND ENERGY, NATURE AND FOREST AGENCY, DIVISION OF FOREST POLICY (1999),
"Denmark: Economic Incentives for the Transformation of Privately Cultivated Forest Areas into Strict (Untouched) Forest Reserves".

DE CIVITA, P. FILION, F., FREHS, J. and JAY, M. (1999),
"The Environmental Valuation Reference Inventory (EVRI) – A New Tool for Benefits Transfers", paper presented at the World Congress of Environmental and Resource Economists, Venice, Italy, 26 June, 1998.

EHRLICH, P.R. and EHRLICH, A.H. (1992),
"The Value of Biodiversity", *Ambio*, 21(3), pp. 219-226.

FILION. F. and ADAMOWICZ, W. (1994),
"Socio-economic Valuation of Biodiversity", in *Biodiversity in Canada: A Science Assessment*, Environment Canada, Ottawa, Canada, pp. 221-242.

*FILION, F, FREHS, F. and SPRECHER, D. (1999),
"Revealing the Economic Value of Biodiversity: A New Incentive Measure to Conserve and Protect It".

FISHER, A.C. and HANEMANN, W.M. (1987),
"Quasi-Option Value: Some Misconceptions Dispelled", *Journal of Environmental Economics and Environmental Management*, 14, pp. 183-190.

FREEMAN, A.M. III. (1993),
The Measurement of Environmental and Resource Values: Theory and Methods, Resources for the Future, Washington DC.

*GUDMUNDSSON E., KEPPLER, J.H., and SUTINEN, J. (1998),
"Individual Transferable Quotas as an Incentive Measure for the Conservation and the Sustainable Use of Marine Biodiversity".

HANNA, S. and MUNASINGHE, M. (eds) (1995),
Property Rights and the Environment: Social and Ecological Issues, The World Bank, Washington DC.

*HARLEY, D. and DAVIES, R.C. (1999),
"Heathland Management in the UK".

*HEIMLICH, R.E., WIEBE, K. CLAASSEN R. and GADSBY, D. (1999),
"US Experiences with Incentive Measures to Promote the Conservation of Wetlands".

HIGH-LEVEL ADVISORY GROUP ON THE ENVIRONMENT (1997),
Guiding the Transition to Sustainable Development: The Report of the High-Level Advisory Group on the Environment to the Secretary-General of the Organisation for Economic Co-operation and Development, OECD, Paris.

*HOPPICHLER, J. and GROIER, M. (1999),
"The Austrian Programme on Environmentally Sound and Sustainable Agriculture: Experiences and Consequences of Sustainable Use of Biodiversity in Austrian Agriculture".

*HUBACEK, K. and BAUER, W. (1999),
"Economic Incentive Measures in the Creation of the National Park Neusiedler See – Seewinkel", Technical Report, Federal Environmental Agency, Vienna.

*HUTCHING, G. (1999),
"New Zealand: Conservation of the Pae O Te Rangi Area".

IUCN (1995),
Best Practice for Conservation Planning in Rural Areas, IUCN, Gland.

*MAGNUSSEN, K. and RYMOEN, E. (1999),
"Valuation of Benefits Connected to Conservation or Improvement of Environmental Quality in Local Watercourses in Norway", Stiftelsen Østfoldforskning, Fredrikstad, Norway.

*MEXICAN MINISTRY OF THE ENVIRONMENT (1999),
"Indications Économiques pour la Protection des Espèces de la Vie Sauvage au Mexique: Le Cas de l'Espèce Ovis canadensis".

*NASKALI, A. (1999),
"Finland: The Act on the Financing of Sustainable Forestry and the Development of Forest Certification".

OECD (1992),
Market and Government Failures in Environmental Management: Wetlands and Forests, OECD, Paris.

OECD (1994),
The Contribution of Amenities to Rural Development, OECD, Paris.

OECD (1995),
St. Petersburg Guidelines on Environmental Funds in the Transition to a Market Economy, OECD, Paris.

OECD (1996),
Saving Biological Diversity: Economic Incentives, OECD, Paris.

169

OECD (1997a),
   "Incentive Measures to Promote the Conservation and the Sustainable Use of Biodiversity: Framework for Case Studies", General Distribution Document, OECD/GD(97)125, OECD, Paris.

OECD (1997b),
   Investing in Biological Diversity: The Cairns Conference, OECD, Paris.

OECD(1997c),
   Environmental Benefits of Agriculture: Issues and Policies, OECD, Paris.

OECD (1997d),
   OECD Environmental Compendium 1997, OECD, Paris.

OECD (1997e),
   Agricultural Policies in OECD Countries: Measurement of Support and Background Information 1997, OECD, Paris.

OECD (1998a),
   "A Strategy for Further OECD Work on Sustainable Development (Note by the Secretary-General), C(98) 46, OECD, Paris.

OECD (1998b),
   Towards Sustainable Development: Environmental Indicators, OECD, Paris.

OECD (1998c),
   "The Implications of the Kyoto Protocol for the Agricultural Sector", COM/ENV/EPOC/AGR/CA(98)55, OECD, Paris.

OECD (1998d),
   Improving the Environment through Reducing Subsidies, OECD, Paris.

OECD (1998e),
   Swapping Debt for the Environment: the Polish EcoFund, OECD, Paris.

OECD (1999a, forthcoming),
   Indicators for Sustainable Agriculture: the York Workshop, OECD, Paris.

OECD (1999b, forthcoming),
   Economic Instruments for Pollution Control and Natural Resources Management in OECD Countries, OECD, Paris.

OECD (1999c, forthcoming),
   Survey on Environmental Funds in CEEC and NIS Countries, OECD, Paris.

PEARCE, D.W.P., et al. (1994),
   Blueprint 3: Measuring Sustainable Development, Earthscan, London.

PEARCE, D.W. and MARKANDYA, A. (1989),
   Environmental Policy Benefits: Monetary Valuation, OECD, Paris.

PEARCE, D.W., MARKANDYA, A. and BARBIER, E.B. (1989),
   Blueprint for a Green Economy, Earthscan Publications, London.

PERRINGS, C. (1991),
   "Reserved Rationality and the Precautionary Principle: Technological Change, Time and Uncertainty in Environmental Decision Making" in R. Costanza (ed.), *Ecological Economics: The Science and Management of Sustainability*, Columbia University Press, New York.

PERRINGS, C., FOLKE, C. and MALER, K-G. (1992),
"The Ecology and Economics of Biodiversity Loss: The Research Agenda", *Ambio*, 21(3), pp. 201-211.

PIGOU, A. C. (1920),
The Economics of Welfare, MacMillan, London.

*PLANNING DIVISION, NATURE CONSERVATION BUREAU, JAPANESE ENVIRONMENT AGENCY (1999),
"The Case of Oze Area: Case Study on the Japanese Experience Concerning Economic Aspects of Conserving Biodiversity".

*POLISH MINISTRY OF ENVIRONMENTAL PROTECTION, NATURAL RESOURCES AND FORESTRY (1999),
"The Implementation of Economic Incentive Measures to Promote the Conservation and Sustainable Use of Biodiversity in the Biebrza Valley, with Special Attention to the Biebrza National Park".

*POPP, D. (1999),
"UNESCO Biosphere Reserves Schorfheide-Chorin and Rhön".

RENARD, V. (1998),
"Application of Tradable Permits to Land-Use Management", ENV/EPOC/GEEI(98)15, OECD, Paris.

*RUBEC, C. (1999),
"Using the Income Tax Act of Canada to Promote Biodiversity and Sensitive Lands Conservation".

*SHIN, H. J. and SHON, H.M. (1999),
"Korean Experiences Relating to the Conservation of Biodiversity in Mount Chiri with Special Attention to the Poaching of Bears".

SMITH, S. (1998),
"The Compatability of Tradable Permits with Other Environmental Policy Instruments", ENV/EPOC/GGEI(98)18, OECD, Paris.

*SPYROPOULOU, S. and DIMOPOULOS, D. (1999),
"Incentives for the Conservation of the Nesting Grounds of the Sea Turtle *Caretta caretta* in Laganas Bay, Zakynthos, Greece".

UNEP (1994),
Convention on Biological Diversity, UNEP, Geneva.

UNITED NATIONS CONFERENCE ON ENVIRONMENT AND DEVELOPMENT (1992),
Rio Declaration on Environment and Development.

WORLD RESOURCES INSTITUTE (1996),
World Resources 1996-97, Oxford University Press, New York.

YOUNG, M. D. and GUNNINGHAM, N. (1997),
"Mixing Instruments and Institutional Arrangements for Optimal Biodiversity Conservation", in OECD, *Investing in Biological Diversity: The Cairns Conference*, OECD, Paris.

171|

OECD PUBLICATIONS, 2, rue André-Pascal, 75775 PARIS CEDEX
PRINTED IN FRANCE
(97 1999 05 1 P) ISBN 92-64-17059-6 – No. 50699 1999